EASY MILES
NO STEPS, NO STILES
– in & around the Lake District

John Barwise
&
Harriet Sharkey

Published by Sigma Leisure – an imprint of
Sigma Press, 5 Alton Road, Wilmslow, Cheshire SK9 5DY, England.

British Library Cataloguing in Publication Data
A CIP record for this book is available from the British Library.

ISBN:978-1-85058-841-2 (13 digit); 1-85058-841-4(10 digit)

Typesetting and Design by: Sigma Press, Wilmslow, Cheshire.

Cover photograph: footpath at Elter Water *(John Barwise)*

Maps: Bute Cartographics. We are grateful to *The Westmorland Gazette* for allowing us to base our maps on those that first appeared in their 'Miles without Stiles' features.

Printed by: Bell & Bain Ltd, Glasgow

Disclaimer: the information in this book is given in good faith and is believed to be correct at the time of publication. No responsibility is accepted by either the authors or publisher for errors or omissions, or for any loss or injury howsoever caused. Only you can judge your own fitness, competence and experience, and the accessibility of each individual route depending on your unique needs. Do not rely solely on sketch maps for navigation: we strongly recommend the use of appropriate Ordnance Survey (or equivalent) maps.

Preface

Easy Miles

This book came about following the enthusiastic response to our accessible walking routes published in South Lakeland's *Westmorland Gazette* in 2003-2005. *Easy Miles* is for everybody who saved the newspaper pages and for people who didn't, yet would like something that's easy to carry and use, wherever they're heading.

Some of our readers suggested routes included in this book. Other routes were recommended to us by the Lake District National Park Authority and the National Trust; others are our own personal favourites.

Who's it for?

The routes are ideal for pushchairs, most wheelchair users and anyone who wants an easy stroll, *whatever the weather*. The beauty of the Lake District and the valleys, fells and estuaries beyond its boundaries is there for everyone to enjoy. Yet, families with young children and people who cannot navigate rocky, gated or steep paths often feel restricted to a few short routes and public parks. This isn't because the wider countryside is impossible to navigate – rather it is due to poor information. *Easy Miles* opens up the countryside and lets you know in advance that the routes are accessible. It features over 30 gentle walks uninterrupted by steps, stiles, gates or other obstacles.

What makes the walks special?

The emphasis for these walks is on accessibility, enjoyment and inspiration. The areas we explore appeal to us – and we hope to you – for their views, wildlife interest, local history, landscape features, or their unique geology and geography. Many lie within the boundaries of the Lake District National Park; those outside the park are in areas of outstanding natural beauty or special scientific interest (SSSI). Most walks include a pub, café or other refreshment point and many are accessible using public transport.

Acknowledgements

The beginnings of Easy Miles came when Harriet Sharkey established the 'Miles without Stiles' walking routes on the back page of *Westmorland Gazette* Leisure Section in September 2003. At the National Trust we'd particularly like to thank Ed Forrest, warden for the Coniston area. Thank you also to Sue

Hotchkiss from the Furness Greenways Partnership, who joined us walks on the Furness Peninsula. The Greenways and Quiet roads initiative is dedicated to developing a network of multi-user non-vehicular routes throughout the Furness peninsula and create links into the Lake District. The Partnership is comprised of representatives from the County Council, Barrow Borough Council and South Lakeland District Council as well as other major stake-holders. Others who have welcomed and supported us include Mirehouse (Keswick) and the residents and wardens of Holehird (Windermere).

Thanks too to all the people who joined us and helped us discover which walks were accessible as well as enjoyable ... particularly Don, Ang, Sam and Josie; Barney, Lucy and family; Jenny and Adam in Ulverston. Above all, we'd like to thank our own families for walking with us and for love and support in helping this book come to life.

John Barwise and Harriet Sharkey

Contents

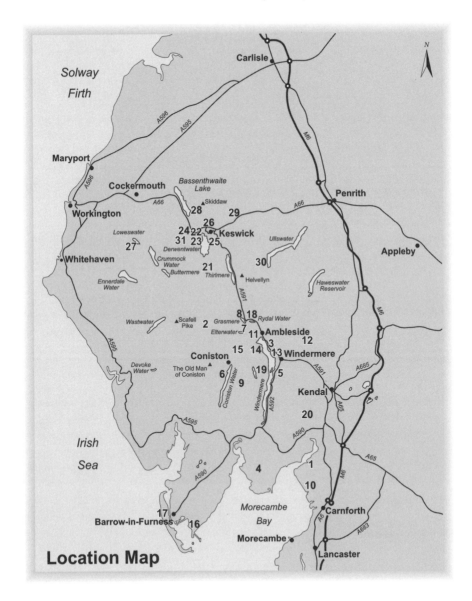

Location Map

Introduction

England's Lake District

Sculpted over millions of years, the mountains, rivers, lakes, valleys and coastline are what make the Lake District and surrounding countryside special, inspiring generations of poets, artists, writers and musicians who have spent time in this tranquil corner of England. The list of famed writers still draws people to the area: Wordsworth, whose house and grave are part of Grasmere's history; De Quincey, the 'opium eater' who romanticised hills and valleys; and Beatrix Potter, whose house in Sawrey looks today just as it did in the sketches she drew over a hundred years ago. Their legacy is followed by many artists today, who display their art in local galleries, or incorporate it into the landscape, as at Grizedale.

Outstanding natural beauty

Cumbria has an amazingly diverse natural ecology. Many of the thousands of species of plants and trees, mosses, grasses and plants are unique to this area and reflect its wide variety of terrain, which encompasses bogs, wood-

Blea Tarn – surrounded by mountains

land, flood plains, glacial valleys, limestone outcrops, shorelines and moorland. Such diversity provides a rich habitat for all kinds of wildlife. Cumbria is the only place in England with wild herds of deer; there are fell ponies too. The rare and very shy bittern is a resident at Leighton Moss Bird Reserve and there are nesting osprey on the crags above Bassenthwaite Lake. Then there are smaller species such as the natterjack toad and great crested newt, which live in some of the small tarns and raised bogs of Cumbria.

Some wildlife habitats have been given special protection because they are unique and irreplaceable. These include, among others, sites of special scientific interest (SSSIs), areas of outstanding natural beauty (AONBs), special areas of conservation (SAC) and coastal areas internationally recognised under the Ramsar Convention on wetlands. It's a delight to spend time in and around these precious corners of our countryside. Some sites require special access permission, but others are open to the public and a number have accessible paths that are featured in the Easy Miles series.

Treading lightly

The Cumbrian countryside is nature's garden and many farmers depend on it for their livelihood. There are a few commonsense things to consider when venturing out:

◆ Take care not to damage, destroy or remove plants, shrubs or even rocks – these are wildlife habitats

◆ Remember that designated areas such as SSSIs and AONBs are specially protected

◆ Don't feed or get too close to wild animals or farm animals.

◆ Leave nothing but footprints – take litter home and leave picnic areas clean and tidy.

◆ Don't light fires, which can seriously damage wildlife habitats and crops.

◆ Always keep dogs under control. Many areas are home to ground nesting birds, such as skylarks and curlews; and in lambing season dogs must be kept on a lead.

Whatever the weather

Most of the routes in this guide are low-level walks on firm ground with occasional gentle slopes. While most people prefer a dry, bright day for a walk, the routes we have chosen are just as much fun in the rain, or even when it's windy or snowing. We've chosen some routes with the changeable Cumbrian weather in mind: those through woods or beside water are particularly suited to rainy days.

Staying safe

Although the routes described here do not take you out into the true wilderness, it is still worth taking a few precautions before you set off: just to stay on the safe side.

◆ Always tell someone where you are going.

◆ Know where you are and follow the paths at all times – take a compass so you know which way you are heading.

◆ Take note of how long the route is and how long it is likely to take – a rough guide is provided with each walk. But remember, everyone walks at their own pace.

◆ Check out the weather forecast, and remember that the temperature can change dramatically even in the course of a single day. Take waterproofs and warm clothing.

◆ Wear comfortable socks and sensible shoes or boots, preferably with good treads.

◆ Always take a day sack with food and drink supplies, basic First Aid equipment and a torch.

Buying local – sustainable living in Cumbria

There is real concern that our way of living is no longer sustainable. According to some experts we need about three Planet Earths just to sustain our current lifestyle. We don't have that option so what this really means is that our children's future is in the balance unless we all do something now.

One solution is to consume fewer resources. Buying local has two real benefits: it means using less transport (and less energy, with less pollution), which is vital for a healthy environment. It also helps keep rural communities alive by supporting jobs in farming and local businesses.

Cumbria has a strong tradition of supporting its local communities: Farmers' Markets, local crafts and business development are all supported and promoted. This helps sustain the rural economy whilst helping to protect the local environment.

And there's plenty to shout about! Cumberland sausages, for example, have royal approval. There are local and organic delicacies to whet the appetite, and Cumbria's arts and crafts have a worldwide reputation.

So, if you want to sustain rural communities in Cumbria and do your bit for the environment, buy local.

Using this book

We hope you'll find the routes in this book easy to follow. Each walk has its own information section to help you decide your route and plan your walk, including:

◆ Description and directions, with numbered points

◆ Simple maps illustrating the route

◆ Overview of location, terrain and gradients, directions to starting point, refreshment and toilet facilities

◆ The final sections of some walks are not suitable for wheelchairs. Please check the route descriptions when you plan.

We have diligently researched each walk and the facilities nearby. We know, however, that things do change from year to year and even from season to season: café's change hands; toilets close down and are built; car parking facilities can change; bus timetables alter. It's also important to note that some pathways are occasionally damaged, others are extended and some may close temporarily for essential works.

Please use the information here as a guide and use other resources to ensure everything is in place as you plan your day.

Getting around

Every trail has its own transport section giving brief details of useful public transport links, car parks, and directions if you're driving.

The published timetable *Getting Around Cumbria and Lake District*, available from tourist information centres, contains all bus, train and boat services in the National Park and to destinations beyond, as far as Lancaster, Morecambe and Barrow.

Timetables and bus routes may change from time to time. For more up to date more information we recommend you contact the tourist information centre local to your walk or call Traveline on 0870 608 2608.

National organisations that care for the countryside

The Lake District and the wonderful countryside beyond the boundaries of the national park are cared for by private landowners as well as public organisations. Without their dedication, vision and support much of the landscape would change, and certainly many of the routes contained in this book would not be so easily accessible.

LDNPA

The Lake District National Park Authority is responsible for looking after the largest National Park in England, covering fells, lakes, villages, towns and beaches. The LDNPA helps to sustain the unique character of the National Park and actively supports the local communities that live here. Some of the accessible routes in this book have been created and continue to be managed by the National Park Authority. To find out more about their work visit their website: www.lake-district.gov.uk.

National Trust

The National Trust is a charity that oversees some 25% of the Lake District National Park. The National Trust and the National Park Authority work closely together in the Lake District, sharing common interests and complementary objectives. You can get more information by calling 015394 35599 or 0870 4584000 or visiting www.nationaltrust.org.uk.

The Forestry Commission

The Forestry Commission is the state forest service for Great Britain, managing the nation's forests for timber production, recreation, wildlife and conservation and landscape and design. One quarter of the Lake District National Park is managed by the Forestry Commission and there are two Forest Parks here with accessible trails: Grizedale and Whinlatter. Find out more at www.forestry.gov.uk/northwestengland.

RSPB

The RSPB is the largest wildlife conservation charity in Europe. It works to protect threatened species and habitats and to secure a healthy environment for birds and other wildlife. The society owns and manages close to 200 nature reserves in the UK, more than half of which are open to the public. Leighton Moss is one such reserve, providing easily accessible walks for people to get close to nature. Many of the trails and hides on the reserve can be used by people with disabilities, including wheelchair users.

Cumbria Wildlife Trust

This is dedicated to the conservation of wildlife and has over 40 nature reserves across Cumbria including peat bogs, limestone pavements, ancient woodlands and coastal sites. Supported by over 15,000 members, the Trust works in partnership with local communities, landowners and others to conserve, create and protect wildlife habitats and actively campaigns to promote a greater appreciation and understanding of nature throughout Cumbria. For further information please contact 01539 816300. Website: www.cumbriawildlifetrust.org.uk

Furness Greenways Partnership

The Furness Greenways Partnership aims to establish a network of over 60km of multi-user non-vehicular routes throughout the Furness peninsula and with links into the Lake District. The Partnership is comprised of representatives from the County Council, Barrow Borough Council and South Lakeland District Council as well as other major stakeholders, and established the first greenway (on Walney Island, see page 64) in 2000. Further information about Greenways and Quiet Roads can be found at www.countryside.gov.uk/LAR/Recreation/Greenways/index.asp.

Beyond the walks

The walks in this book by no means represent an exhaustive collection of accessible routes in Cumbria; there are more. There's the Cumbrian Way, which meanders through 100km of Lakeland countryside – some of our walks join this route at various points. There are many other ways to enjoy the area too. In addition to the walking routes, accessible options for a day's outing can include open parkland (such as Fell Foot, near Windermere); stately houses (Levens Hall, Holker Hall and Sizergh Castle, to mention just a few); and visitor attractions (like Ostrich World, Wetheriggs Pottery, Lakeside Aquarium and many, many more). Please ask at Tourist Information Centres about accessibility, opening hours and facilities.

1. Arnside: shore trail

Overview: A short coastal route. The concrete path is generally smooth and in good condition with a few minor ruts and cracks.

Distance: About 1km round-trip.

Time: Allow 1 hour

Map and grid reference: OS Explorer OL7. The English Lakes – South-eastern area. Grid reference 454786 at the car park (1)

Gradient: A short descent then generally level over the rest of the route

Refreshments: Beach Walk Café on the trail with Albion Hotel and other facilities on the promenade and in the village.

Toilets: Public toilets in the village

Getting there:

By car: From Milnthorpe take the B5782 to Arnside.

Parking: The car park is on the Promenade close to Albion Hotel.

Public transport: Transpennine Express and Northern Rail both operate a regular coastal train services. Stagecoach operate a regular 552 local bus service to Arnside from Kendal.

About the walk

The picturesque coastal village of Arnside is a wonderful place to take a refreshing stroll – clean salty air coming off the sea, easy walking and plenty to see along this coastal path as it meanders around the bay.

Arnside lies within a designated Area of Outstanding Natural Beauty (AONB) which also takes in Sandside to the north and Silverdale, Warton Crag and Leighton Moss to the south. AONBs are usually defined by their attractive landscape and variety of fauna and flora: the area around Arnside has both in abundance. Limestone hills, mixed deciduous woodland, marshes and grassy meadows provide a range of habitats for a rich variety of wildlife including red squirrels and you might even catch a glimpse of the very rare High Brown Fritillary butterfly as it ventures out from Warton Crag.

Contrast this with the coastal scenery – ever changing as the tides ebb and flow along the estuary. Low tide reveals mile upon mile of mudflats and sand that provide rich pickings for thousands of wading birds and wildfowl from neighbouring Leighton Moss and other parts of the Bay. As the tide turns the scenery changes dramatically, and mudflats quickly disappear as the "tidal

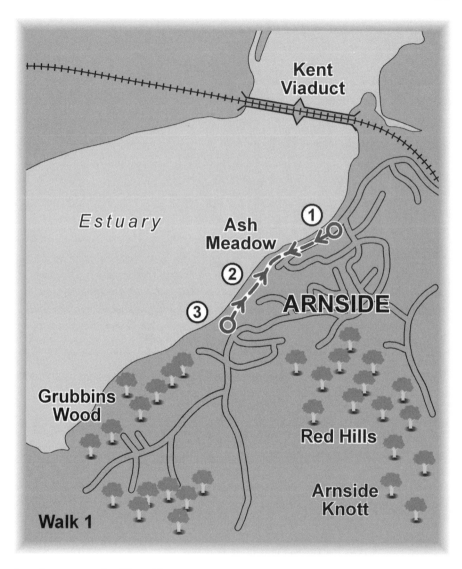

bore" races up the River Kent, swallowing up most of the low-lying features in its path. Only the 1566-foot long viaduct carrying the railway line across Morecambe Bay holds its own against the incoming tide – very exciting to watch.

Arnside – a wonderful place to take a refreshing stroll

The route

This is a short walk leading from the car park (1) at Arnside Promenade stretching out south-west along the coast – it's about 1km round trip. There is a ramp down from the car park and the concrete path continues along the shore past the new Ashmeadows residential development. The path continues along the shore for a few hundred metres before coming to the Beech Walk Café (2). This place is really worth a visit – great food, and lovely views across the estuary. The ascent to the café is very steep for wheelchair users but there is a popular rest spot just below.

The route continues a short way to the new coastguard station and on for a further 250 metres or so (3). Beyond here the path is loose gravel and not suitable for wheelchairs. Also note that this part of the route is subject to flooding at high tides – details of times and heights of tides are posted at Arnside Pier and a siren warns of incoming tide.

2. Blea Tarn: through glacial times

Overview: Generally wide flat path with a few small gradients, suitable for accompanied wheelchair access.

Distance: Less than 3km (2 miles) round trip.

Time: Allow 1 hour

Map and grid reference: OS Explorer OL6. The English Lakes – South-western area. Start point: grid reference 296043.

Gradients: Mostly flat, with gentle inclines in places.

Refreshments: Bring your own

Toilets: None near the route

Getting there:

By car: Take the B5343 from Skelwith Bridge through the Great Langdale valley. After about 8km (5 miles) the road turns sharp left and soon starts to rise steeply up the fell towards Blea Tarn. Follow the road for another 2.5km to the National Trust car park on the left of the road overlooking the tarn (1).

Parking: National Trust car park on the eastern side of the road.

Public transport: There is no public transport available to take you to Blea Tarn although the Langdale Rambler does go to the Dungeon Ghyll pub at the head of Great Langdale.

About the walk

This is an easy walk with great views and a wonderfully restful atmosphere. Blea Tarn is situated on the fells that divide Great Langdale from Little Langdale in the heart of the Lake District. From Great Langdale, the road meanders steeply upwards towards the tarn, offering spectacular views across most of the central fells: Bow Fell, Crinkle Crags, Wetherlam, Wrynose and the magnificent Langdale Pikes are all visible from this road.

Blea Tarn is a protected Site of Special Scientific Interest (SSSI), designated under the Wildlife and Countryside Act. These sites are special because of their unique geological or ecological features. Blea Tarn itself is a classic glacial relic and lies in a shallow trough, cut by huge ice flows that once moved across from Great Langdale down to Little Langdale. Lying virtually undisturbed for thousands of years, sediments at the bottom of the tarn have provided scientists with an unbroken historical timeline of ecological diversity. Peat has now formed over much of the northern part of the trough giving a tranquil open landscape.

The route

The walk starts at the National Trust car park on the east side of the road, over-looking the tarn (1). From here take the footpath down to the southern edge of the tarn, crossing over a wooden bridge (with ramps) (2).

Follow the footpath for a further 0.5km through the woods. Larch, Scots Pine, Silver Birch and Mountain Ash are just a few of the woodland species that you

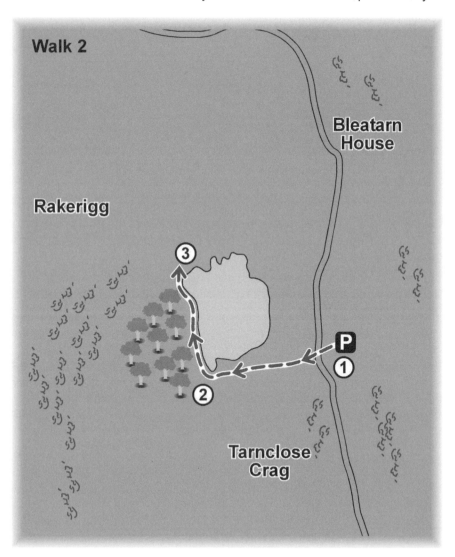

Blea Tarn – a landscape sculpted by glaciers

will find as you go. Continue to the small promontory at the northern edge of the tarn (3). Here the local ecology is very different and is colonised by ferns, reed beds and a variety of grasses.

The area is managed by the National Trust and there are seats along a well-maintained path with plenty of places to picnic and watch the occasional buzzard gliding overhead.

Optional extensions

The footpath continues north for a further 0.5km and eventually rejoins the road leading back to Great Langdale. The path rises gently over this section but it is rough in places and not fully accessible to wheelchairs.

3. Brockhole, Windermere

Overview: Mainly tarmac and compacted gravel surfaces

Distance: 1.5km (1mile)

Time: Allow 2 hours

Map and grid reference: OS Explorer OL7. The English Lakes – South-eastern area. Start point: Brockhole Visitor Car Park (1) – Grid reference: 389010

Gradients: Mostly gentle inclines or level paths with steeper sections up to the visitor centre

Refreshments: Visitor centre tearoom and shop – all with wheelchair access.

Toilets: There are toilets and some have wheelchair access.

Contact details: Brockhole Visitor Centre: 015394 46601

Website: www.lake-district.gov.uk – click on 'Brockhole Visitor Centre'

Getting there:

By car: Brockhole Visitor Centre is just off the A591, 2 miles north of Windermere railway station.

Parking: There is a large car park – there is a small charge

Public transport: Brockhole is on the route of buses 599 (Bowness – Ambleside), 555 (Keswick – Lancaster) and 618 (Ambleside – Barrow). Another stress-free option is to take the leisurely boat service from Ambleside to Brockhole which operates hourly during the summer season.

About the walk

Brockhole is a treasure trove of attractions and nature trails and all just a short walk away from the main visitor centre and café. Owned and managed by the National Park Authority, the 30 acres of gardens and grounds are open throughout the year and are maintained to enhance the natural environment. There are wildflower meadows, yew hedges, terraced gardens and extensive woodland, which all provide the ideal habitat for a rich mix of butterflies, birds and other animals.

Brockhole's adventure playground is open throughout the year and there are other events and activities running from March to October. The visitor centre has a shop, a café and an exhibition area illustrating the unique geology, geography and wildlife of the Lake District: a 30-minute film *'An Introduction to Lakeland'* depicts the rich cultural heritage of the Lake District and its people. For those who want to find out more about the Lake District there's also an Environmental Education Centre that provides a range of courses for different interest groups.

Brockhole provides assistance for wheelchair users including the 'Brockmobile' electric bus for groups, and an electric scooter. There is also an accessible car parking area closer to the Centre.

The route

There are various lakeshore walks, heritage trails and guided walks for people requiring assistance. This one starts from the top of the visitors' car park (1). Follow the tarmac ramp up, then left down the hill behind an archway for about 150 metres to the gate (2). Turn left into the Wildflower Meadows. The

Brockhole offers a treasure trove of nature trails and attractions

adventure playground and picnic tables are just ahead.

Follow the gravel path through the meadows for 100 metres before bearing right. After 150m turn right (3) and continue along the paddock for a further 200 metres. Turn left here (4) and 150 metres further on is the lake shore (5).

Turn left following the shoreline for a further 200 metres (6) – there are seats here and the views across Windermere to the mountains beyond are spectacular. It is possible to continue from here but it is quite steep. The best option is to return back along the shoreline to (4) and from here follow the tarmac path

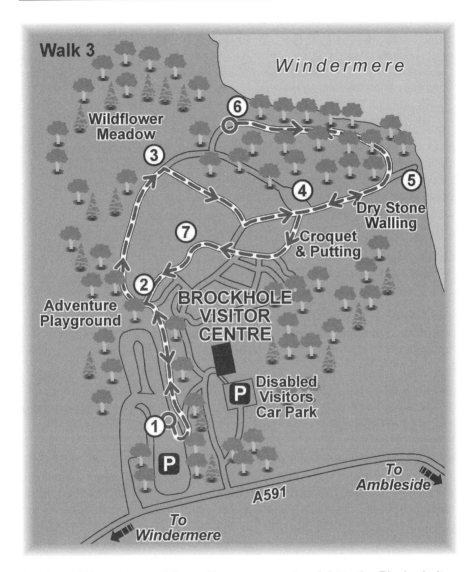

for about 100 metres past the putting green turning right to the Picnic shelter 200 metres further on (7).

The trail from here leads back to the car park. Or, instead, you might want to head up to the Visitor Centre gardens and café – please note that these paths have 1:12 gradients.

4. Cartmel: a day at the races

Overview: The path is mostly tarmac and compacted cobblestone – it's a bit bumpy in places but suitable for wheelchair access.

Distance: About 2.2km (1½ miles)

Time: Allow 2-3 hours

Map and grid reference: OS Explorer OL7. The English Lakes – South-eastern area. Grid reference: 377787 – car park (1)

Gradients: Level ground along most of the trail until you get to the south-west edge of Lane Park wood.

Refreshments: Pubs and other refreshment facilities in Cartmel.

Toilets: At the race track during events (including accessible toilets).

Getting there:

> **By car:** *Cartmel is about 8km south of Newby Bridge. Take the A590 and then follow the signposts.*

> **Parking:** *at the racecourse*

> **Public transport:** *Buses 532 and 530 from Kendal; no buses on Sundays.*

About the walk

The National Hunt racecourse in Cartmel is the starting point for this delightful walk through open fields, meadows and woodland.

Everything about Cartmel's racecourse is unique: it is the smallest National Hunt track in Britain and yet has the longest run-in at just over 4 furlongs long. Augustinian monks are thought to have started the sporting event about eight hundred years ago, racing donkeys round the oval field. It's now part of the national horseracing scene, attracting over 40,000 race goers every year.

Another obvious attraction of this area is Cartmel itself, one of the oldest and most attractive villages in south Lakeland. Its focus is the impressive Priory, founded in 1188 by William Marshal, Baron of Cartmel. The arch of the medieval Gatehouse dates back to 1330 and many local houses date back to the 16th Century.

The route

Our walk starts at the car park (1) on the west of the village just beyond the

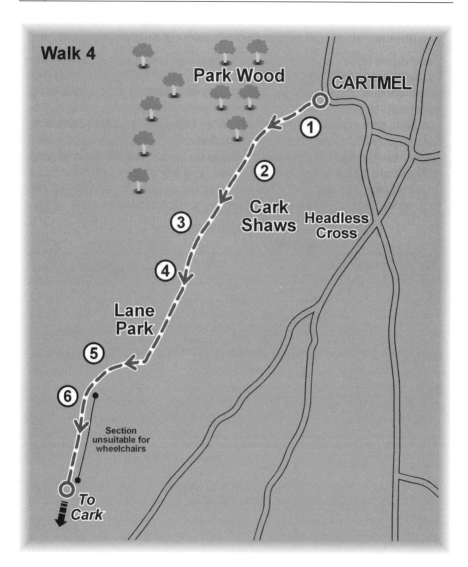

village square. From here the oval racecourse opens up before you. The path through the race course is about 200 metres (2). Continue through a gate with Park Wood on your right and Cark Shaws wood on your left.

You are now in open country with fine views of the surrounding hills. Continue south-west for 200 metres and you will pass Seven Acres (3), a derelict small holding, on your right. Go through the gate and after another 150 metres

Woodland walk – just a stone's throw from Cartmel racecourse

proceed through another gate into Lane Park (4), a mixed deciduous wood-land that offers ideal habitat for a variety of birds and other animals. The River Eea runs parallel to the path at this point, although you may not see it in summer, when the hedgerows grow high. Towards the edge of the wood, a further 100 metres or so, the trail takes you to the right and starts to rise. Unac-companied wheelchair users are advised to return to Cartmel by the same route.

Optional extension

The incline is gentle at first but it gets steeper as you leave Lane Park (5). The trail is uneven and quite steep over the next 150 meters or so. If you wish to continue, the path leads to a fork in the road (6). Taking the left-hand fork will take you along Cistercian Way. This quiet lane continues for about 1km, past Low Bank Side Farm to join the Cark-Cartmel road. Most of this lane is tarmac but there are some muddy and uneven parts. Turning right here will take you into Cark about 100 metres further on.

5. Cockshott Point, Bowness-on-Windermere

Overview: Easy path, muddy at times, and exceptional views.

Distance: 3.2km (2 miles)

Time: Around 1 hour.

Map and grid reference: OS Explorer OL7. The English Lakes – South-eastern area. Start point grid reference 398966.

Gradients: Mild.

Refreshments: Cafés and pubs in Bowness, plus stalls at Ferry Nab (open weekends and holidays).

Toilets: At the Glebe car park, and at Ferry Nab car park; both with wheelchair access (Radar Key needed).

Getting there:

By car: Follow the A592 or A 5074 to Bowness. You can't miss the pier. The Glebe and main car parks are clearly sign posted.

Parking: Car park at the Glebe, spaces along the road, and at Braithwaite Fold Car Park.

Public transport: Regular buses to Bowness from Windermere, Ambleside, Keswick and Kendal arrive close to the Tourist Information Centre. A seasonal shuttle bus runs from Windermere Railway and Bus Station to the Glebe and Braithwaite Fold Car Park.

About the walk

The Lake District's longest lake is stunning from any viewpoint – and at any time of year. This route gives superb views from quiet woodland and open fields.

This is an easy route, particularly for kids, with opportunities to check out small rowing boats and grand yachts, and the ducks pecking around by the shore. And there are fabulous views over the water: northward towards the fells above Troutbeck and to Fairfield Horseshoe beyond Ambleside; across to Belle Isle, with its imposing circular house; westwards to Harrow Slack and the woods behind; and southwards down the lake.

It's surprising that many people who come to Bowness don't stray from the well-beaten track along pavements and shop fronts: the path to Cockshott

Gently sloping grass runs to the lake shore at Cockshott Point

Point offers a perfect balance to chips, ice cream, shopping and Beatrix Potter. You could also combine it with a trip on one of the boats that run up the lake to Waterhead (Ambleside).

The route

This walk is circular, so you could start anywhere. We start at the Glebe Rd Car Park (1). Come out of the car park and turn left, following the pavement with the lakeside shops on your right. Beyond the last shops you'll see a gate, which opens onto a path beneath the trees (2). As you emerge into the fields the path continues straight ahead. To get to Cockshott Point (3) you need to head across the gently sloping grass (sometimes grazed by cows).

Cockshott Point and its small pebbly beach, directly opposite Belle Isle, is a great spot for picnics if the weather allows. From the point, an uneven path follows the lake shore southwards and winds up between rocky crags and majestic old trees. Alternatively, you can back-track across the grass and rejoin the wider path until it emerges from the trees into open pasture and the lake shore. There are several benches here, next to a hedge, which is usually alive with blackbirds and robins, and facing the open lake. From here you can

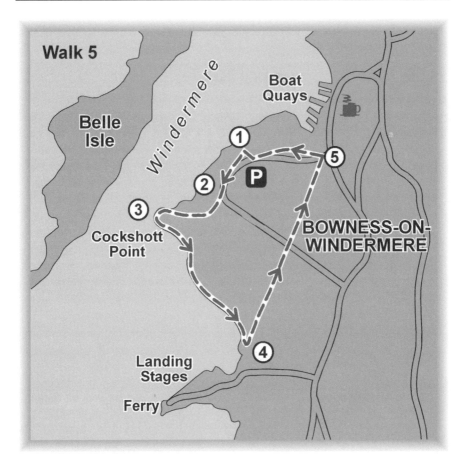

watch ducks and gulls as well as private boats and the car-ferry gliding across the water in the distance. The path continues to a wide wheelchair accessible kissing gate (4).

If you're curious about boats, or wish to stop for some refreshment, turn right into Ferry Nab car park. In winter, scores of boats are moored here. In the summer it's a hive of activity since it gives access to the public launching site.

For the return route to the Glebe, retrace your steps to the kissing gate and onto the slate-dust path that runs across the field to Glebe Road. Cross the road (usually fairly quiet) and head straight on into Rectory Road, which is very quiet, because vehicles are prohibited. This will take you past churchyard and grassland, with more fine views, to the tourist information centre in Bowness (5). From here, you could continue into Bowness for refreshments, shopping or sightseeing, or turn left along Glebe Road, with the lake on your right, to return to your starting point.

Optional extension

If you want to stay out for longer you can combine this walk with a ferry-hop on the Cross-Lakes Shuttle to the west shore of the lake and a further 4km stroll (see page 34).

6. Coniston Water: a lake shore stroll

Overview: Wide flat path.

Distance: 5km (3 miles) return journey.

Time: 1½ hours.

Map and grid reference: OS Explorer OL7. The English Lakes –
South-eastern area. Start point grid reference 308970.

Gradients: Mostly flat, with very slight inclines in places.

Refreshments: Café by the jetty.

Toilets: Beside the car park, with wheelchair access.

Getting there:

By car: Take the A593 to Coniston then, on the south side of the town,
follow Lake Road to the lake shore.

Parking: Coniston Boating Centre. LDNPA car parking at the end of
Lake Road, by the jetty, with parking bays for wheelchair users.

Public transport: Public buses to Coniston drop off in the village
centre, from where it's a short walk to the Boating Centre. The 'Cross
Lakes Shuttle' links Coniston with Ambleside, Hawkshead and
Windermere and drops at the Waterhead Hotel, which has a ferry
launch: you could take the ferry to the boating centre (1) or to the jetty at
the end of the walk (3).

Boats: These run regularly between the Jetty and Brantwood, on the
opposite shore, and to the north and south of the lake. Call 015394
36216 for information on sailing times and accessibility. For self-hire
rowing and electrically powered boats, call the Boating Centre on
015394 41366.

About the walk

This walk affords great views over Coniston Water and the surrounding fells,
and it takes you through history – past Coniston Hall and across land once
used for charcoal burning and iron working; the iron ore produced after burning was shipped down the lake. Today, you'll be spoilt for choice for places to
stop, rest and picnic. If you're with children, they will no doubt want to stop by
the lake and in the woods to explore and play – you could spend most of the
day wandering this path.

You could combine this walk with a trip on the Gondola across the lake to

There are many beaches on this route, giving fine views across Coniston Water

Brantwood, erstwhile home of John Ruskin, art lover, naturalist, philosopher and social reformer. You can also hire a rowing, motor or sailing boat and enjoy the water at your leisure.

The route

Begin at the car park by the jetty (1) and follow Lake Road back towards the village, past the retail/industrial units. The road bends sharply to the left and crosses a bridge. After the bridge you'll see a double kissing gate wide enough for chairs. If you have come by bus, follow Lake Road from the village side until you reach this gate.

Once through the gate, you join the path that runs across fields flecked with sheep. It takes a sharp left turn (2) onto a wider track towards Coniston Hall and the lake. Coniston Hall, with medieval origins and the striking thick and stumpy Flemish chimneys visible for miles, was renovated by the National Trust in the 1970s. It's the focal point for Coniston Hall farm and campsite. If you're lucky, you may spot peacocks as you pass through the grounds.

From the hall, follow the main track south. It takes you through the fields that are used for camping in the summer. Take the second left turn off the track, with a small copse of trees on your right, and go through a wicket gate which

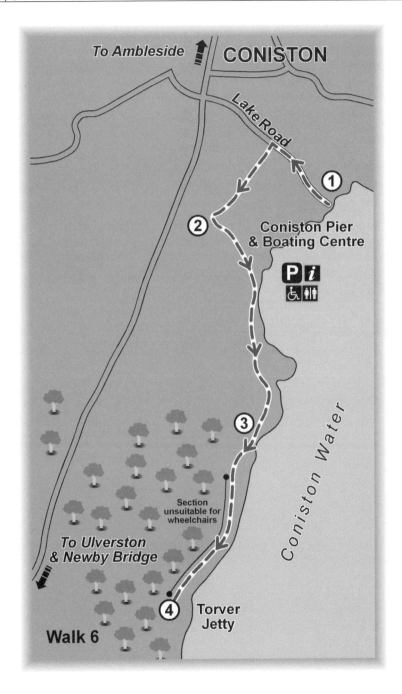

Walk 6

brings you to the lake shore, with its pebbly beaches and grassy banks. Across the water you can see Brantwood, former home of John Ruskin, and you may see SY *Gondola* gliding majestically up and down the lake. The path continues along the shore and then goes through a double kissing gate onto Hoathwaite, a working National Trust farm, and another campsite where large oak trees line the shore (3). This is an ideal spot for a picnic.

Optional extension

Flooding in this area can cause erosion, making the path trickier to navigate from here on. Beyond Hoathwaite the path is very rough and accessible only for robust, off-road wheelchairs. The return route runs back the way you came.

For those particularly determined, the route could continue another 200 yards through woodland to Torver Jetty (4), from where a boat runs back to the main boat launch at the boating centre – a nice way to finish off. If you'd like to pick up the boat, you'll need to request the special stop with the Launch centre at Lake Road jetty before setting off.

7. Elterwater:
even better when it's raining!

Overview: Generally wide flat path with a few small gradients, suitable for accompanied wheelchair access. There are a couple of gates en route.

Distance: 4km (2½ miles) return journey on linear path .

Time: Allow 2½ hours for return trip.

Map and grid reference: OS Explorer OL7. The English Lakes – South-eastern area. Start point Elterwater car park, grid reference 328047.

Gradients: Mostly flat, with gentle inclines in places.

Refreshments: Britannia Inn at Elterwater and Coffee shop and Hotel at Skelwith Bridge.

Toilets: No public facilities.

Getting there

By car: From Ambleside take the A593. At Skelwith Bridge turn right and follow the B5343 to Elterwater.

Parking: Pay and display car park in the village, near the bridge.

Public transport: The Langdale Rambler 516 runs from Ambleside six times a day to the Skelwith Bridge Hotel and Elterwater.

About the walk

Elterwater village to Skelwith Bridge is a walk that is full of interest and surprise and a classic 'whatever the weather' type of trail.

The trail follows Great Langdale Beck between semi-natural woodland on your left and open grazing fields on your right. Ahead of you is the wide stretch of open countryside which draws you to the shores of Elter Water. From here there are fabulous views back up the valley to the Langdale Pikes towering in the distance.

There's nothing more exciting than a traditional Lakeland downpour and watching nature's drainage system kick into action, and if you can make it to this location on a rainy day (with waterproof clothing of course), you won't regret it. Great Langdale Beck frequently gives a spectacular display as it tumbles and rushes towards Elter Water. On the fells around, gentle mountain streams can turn into angry rivers that may even breach stone walls as they race with gravity to the valley bottoms and lakes.

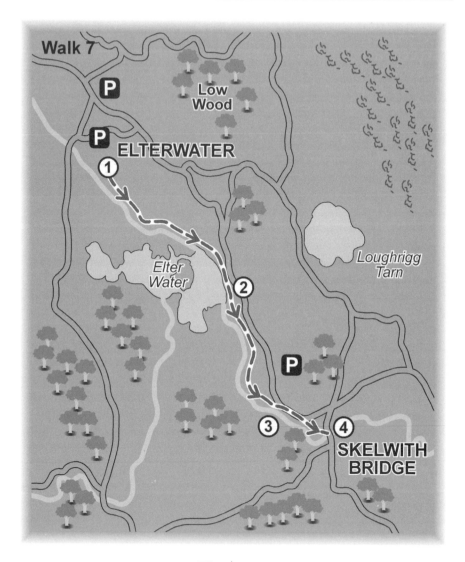

The route

The walk starts next to the car park (1), shadowing Great Langdale Beck for about 1km (0.6m) before linking up with the Cumbria Way. This then takes you through mixed woodland for about 0.5 km and down to the grassy shores of Elter Water (2). On dry days, these shores are perfect for picnicking; if it's raining you're better off taking a break under cover in the woods.

A gentle stroll past Elter Water, whatever the weather.

The trail gradually moves away from Elter Water rising slightly to a gate and on through more woodland for around 0.5 km (3). From this point the path is unsuitable for wheelchairs at present. You can choose to join the B5343 road for the 300 metre walk to Skelwith Bridge (4) or return back along the footpath to the car park at Elterwater village. This section of road to Skelwith Bridge has no pavement and can be quite busy with traffic during the holiday season.

Optional extension

You may want to continue along the footpath from (3) to the powerful Skelwith Force waterfall, which is a fantastic sight, especially when the river is in spate. Unfortunately this section is unsuitable for wheelchairs.

8. Grasmere: a riverside walk

Overview: Easy tarmac surface beside the river, followed by a saunter through the village.

Distance: 2km (1¼ miles)

Time: Roughly half an hour one way; total time depends on how long you spend shopping or sipping coffee.

Map and grid reference: OS Explorer OL7. The English Lakes – South-eastern area. Start point grid reference: 337077.

Gradients: Flat.

Refreshments: Cafés and pubs in Grasmere.

Toilets: In the centre of village at the village green, including disabled access; toilets in Stock Lane Car Park open spring-summer.

Getting there:

> *By car: Grasmere is on the B5287, accessible from the A591 which runs between Keswick and Ambleside.*

> *Parking: Car park at each end of the walk and in the centre of the village. Parking in the school yard at weekends and holidays for a small donation (for the school fund).*

> *Public transport: Regular buses to Grasmere from Keswick, Ambleside, Windermere and Kendal. Bus stop opposite Craglands shop and at the village green.*

About the walk

Grasmere's riverside path is a short, picturesque route that lends added interest to an already charming village. Grasmere nestles amid some of the grandest fells in the central Lake District and has a mêlée of shops, cafés and pubs that make it a tempting place to stop for at least a day. It's also popular as Wordsworth's chosen home and his final resting place.

This route is good for even the most reluctant of young children since the river, surrounding fields and distant fells offer constant interest, there is a play park at one end, and the shops are enticing. The path is wide enough for two or three to walk abreast, or for a single wheelchair, and along its entire route it is lined with a fence and tapping rail designed to guide people with impaired vision.

The Millennium Bridge crosses the river beneath the shade of overhanging trees

The route

Begin at Broadgate LDNPA car park (1) next to the village hall and play park, where you'll find an information plaque about the route. The path begins by crossing the river. On a clear day, it reflects the whale-like curves of Dollywagon and Fairfield, high fells rising above Stone Arthur to the north-east. After crossing the bridge, the path winds between flat fields spread across the valley bottom and the backs of Grasmere's houses, shops and cafés. The river between the two harbours a number of birds – the ubiquitous ducks, dippers, wagtails and even king fishers.

About two-thirds of the way along the route (2) is the Millennium Bridge (see picture above). Once you have crossed it, bear to the right. The path takes you through the grounds of Grasmere Village School and emerges into the village opposite Craglands shop (3).

For the return route, turn right along the pavement. When you see the church, turn right to cut through the church yard. William Wordsworth is buried here, along with other members of his family. The exit to the church is marked by the

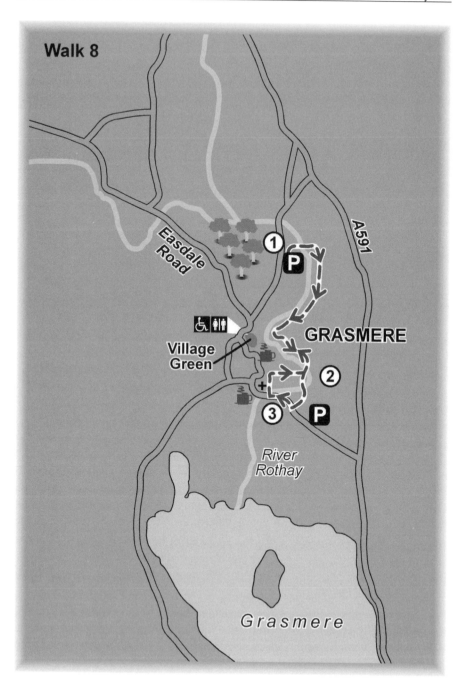

arched lynch gate and the tempting smell of unique Grasmere Gingerbread, cooked to a secret recipe unchanged for centuries.

After about 10 yards, turn right onto a wide track. This leads you back to the Millennium Bridge and you can follow the riverside path back to the start point. Alternatively, you can make your way back to Broadgate car park through the village.

Optional extension

If you would like to go further you could follow Easedale Road opposite the village green into Easedale Valley. The road is used by cars but is usually pretty quiet and there is passing space. Where the road ends a tarmac track runs along the flat bed of the valley, with Sourmilk Gill tumbling over the rocky fellside ahead. There is no destination as such, but if you want the extra stretch this round trip to the end of the lane and back into the village would take 1½ – 2 hours.

9. Grizedale Ridding Wood:
Art in the forest

Overview: A blend of tarmac and fine gravel path specially adapted for wheelchairs. Mostly flat, some slight inclines.

Distance: 2km (1¼ miles)

Time: 1 – 1½ hrs; though you could easily spend a day in the forest.

Map and grid reference: OS Explorer OL7. The English Lakes – South-eastern area. Grid reference 336943

Gradients: Mostly flat, a few very slight gradients.

Refreshments: Café at the Grizedale Centre.

Toilets: At the car parks, accessible.

Getting there:

By car: The best route into Grizedale is via Hawkshead. From Hawkshead village, head south towards lakeside and, 500m after the school, turn left up a steep hill. This road, single track in places, runs straight to the visitor centre and car parks. Coaches must access Grizedale via a longer route to avoid narrow and steep bends: please contact the centre for directions.

Parking: At Start of Walk at Grizedale Hall and at Grizedale Forest Centre.

Public transport: The Cross-Lakes Shuttle (525) from Bowness Pier 3, Hawkshead or Coniston Pier runs at weekends, school holidays and daily throughout July, august and September (call 015394 45161 for details).

About the walk

This is one of our favourite short routes in Grizedale, a managed forest criss-crossed by many paths, cycle routes and tracks. You could enjoy this as part of a longer day in the forest. The Ridding Wood Trail has been specially designed with children, wheelchair users, art lovers and families in mind – it's easy to follow and is dotted with sculptures. There are also great views across the wide valley bottom towards the hills beyond. In spring, the trees are particularly superb and bluebells carpet the ground. This is a good walk at any time of day, but best in the evening when the route is bathed in the golden glow of the setting sun. It's also good in drizzle or light rain, as it is sheltered in most parts by the trees.

The route

Begin at Grizedale Hall car park (1). With the old buildings on your left, follow the wide tarmac path, which soon passes beneath a curved wooden sculpture. Look out for uniquely carved benches, hogs in the hedges and other woodland animals. The path crosses a small stream and then bends to the right. On the left, the bank rises steeply. To the right, the view takes in the

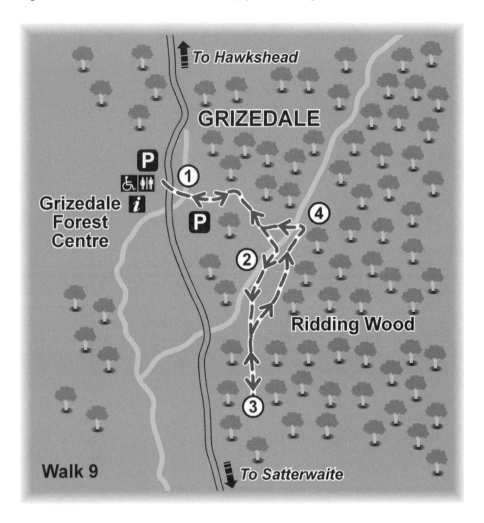

Sculptures on the trail: a chance to add music to the forest

valley: in the mature copper beech you may notice a large steel circle. This is 'Ting', a sculpture woven through the tree's branches 20 years ago by Colin Rose.

A few yards further on are the musical sculptures – great fun for kids and adults alike, with the chance to fill the trees with woody echoes. At the covered shelter, which gives the impression that the forest floor is growing above your head, the path bends to the left. Follow the bridge (2) high above the river, and stick to the path as it curves to the right. Small paths lead up and into the woods from here: one is lined with curled up wooden sculptures, giant fern spores that make perfect seats for small children. Further along you'll come to a beetle-carved seat. A little way past this cast your eyes high into the trees on the right – there is a beehive, created by Jony Easterby, that flickers with sparkling lights powered by sunlight.

The track eventually emerges from the tree cover to open grassland. A large curved seat made by Nigel Ross is perfect for taking in the view and a little further the Grizedale Mosaic (3), made by Rosalind Wates in 1992, offers fun for children as they guess what animals are depicted.

On the way back, follow the left branch of the path. You'll pass more sculptures, including fairy-tale houses and carved benches, before meeting Reece Ingram's friendly-looking sheep, and passing beneath the bridge. Here the path runs beside the river, which often tempts children in for a paddle. It runs to a miniature slate-roofed house (4) before climbing with a gentle incline back to the sheltered seat. From here, the path returns to the car park.

Optional extension

Grizedale Forest is managed by Forest Enterprise, and it doubles as an open-air leisure centre, where you could well find yourself spoilt for choice. As well as events through the year (mainly summer) new art works are commissioned on an ongoing basis. Some are temporary, others become part of the landscape, and you could walk all day and still see only a selection of what's on offer. There's also an adventure playground which has been designed with accessibility a priority; a shop; refreshments; and cycle hire (with tag-along trailers for parents with young children).

10. Leighton Moss RSPB Nature Reserve

Overview: Compacted gravel paths suitable for accompanied wheelchair users.

Distance: These are linear paths – the return trip from visitor centre to Griesdale Hide and back again is about 2km (1¼ miles)

Time: Allow 1½ hours – more if you spend time in the hides

Map and grid reference: OS Explorer OL7. The English Lakes – South-eastern area. Start at visitor centre (1), grid reference: 477752.

Gradients: Level paths across the reserve (with one steep section at the beginning of the trail) and ramps with gentle inclines into the hides.

Refreshments: Tearoom and shop (with chair lift to the tearoom)

Toilets: Toilets with wheelchair access

Other facilities: The Reserve also has a range of education facilities.

Free access: Access to the reserve is free if you arrive by public transport or bicycle. There is also free access for those accompanying wheelchair users.

Contact details: RSPB Leighton Moss: Myers Farm, Silverdale, Carnforth, LA5 0SW Tel: 01524 701601 Fax : 01524 702092 E-mail: Leighton.moss@rspb.org.uk; wbsite: www.rspb.org.uk

Getting there:

> **By car:** *Leighton Moss is next to Silverdale railway station and about 2km west of Silverdale*
>
> **Parking:** *Opposite the Visitor Centre*
>
> **Public transport:** *550 bus runs from Kendal to Silverdale twice a day. Trains operate regularly between Carnforth and Barrow in Furness, stopping at Silverdale station. There is also a bittern bus that runs on a Sunday from Lancaster through Carnforth, Leighton Moss and on to Arnside. For more information contact: Carnforth Connect on 01524 734311*

About the walk

The RSPB Leighton Moss nature reserve provides a variety of nature trails with easy access and a great opportunity to watch nature up close from a secluded hide.

At Leighton, there are four hides with wheelchair access

Situated in the shallow marshes that separate land from sea this vast open landscape is a diverse mix of mudflats, lagoons and reed beds and forms part of the largest intertidal zone – between high and low tides – in Britain. It's perhaps hardly surprising that Leighton Moss is teeming with wildlife: it boasts over 80 different species of breeding birds and hosts a quarter of a million ducks and geese each winter; Roe and Red Deer also live here. The Reserve is a protected Site of Special Scientific Interest (SSSI) and sits on the edge of Morecambe Bay, which itself has international recognition under the Ramsar Convention on Wetlands of International Importance.

Leighton Moss is very popular and well equipped. There are two wheelchairs for use around the reserve and the staff will go out of their way to help: ask for a copy of their colourful trail guides to decide where you want to go and check out the 'What's About' white board to see which birds to look out for each day.

The route

The facilities at Leighton Moss are excellent. There are eight hides, four with wheelchair access – all with fantastic views. The paths are of compacted gravel and generally on level ground.

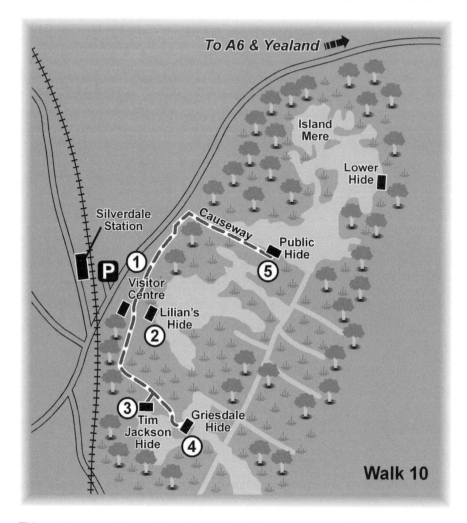

To A6 & Yealand ▮▮▶

Island
Mere

Lower
Hide ▮

Silverdale
Station

Causeway

Public
Hide
⑤

Ⓟ ①
Visitor
Centre

Lilian's
Hide
②

③ Tim
Jackson
Hide
④

Griesdale
Hide

Walk 10

This route covers three of the four Hides with ramp access. Starting at the visitor centre (1) head for the gravel path that leads into the reserve. The first section is rather steep – it is passable for wheelchairs but, if you need help, just ask the staff at the visitor centre. Turning left takes you to Lilian's Hide with views over open water and reedbeds. Look out for Mallard, tufted duck, coot, widgeon, teal and mute swan – you might even catch a glimpse of the reserve's most celebrated resident – the extremely rare and shy bittern. From here head back along the path following the stream on your right and reedbeds on your left, turning right after about 400 metres towards Tim Jackson Hide or carry on to the Griesdale Hide about another 600 metres further on.

You might also want to head over to the Public Hide (5) north-east of the visitor centre. Scurrying about in the woodland fringes, hedges and feeding sites are finches, tits and thrushes – keep your eyes peeled for marsh harriers flying over the reedbeds and the occasional peregrine falcon. All the hides have well positioned viewing platforms and seats so you can take your time here and just enjoy the birds and scenery for as long as you like.

11. Pelter Bridge, Ambleside: to Rydal in Wordsworth's footsteps

Overview: Easy tarmac surface; quiet road; optional stony track for return.

Distance: 2.5km (1½ miles) one way, with option of return by bus for those without wheelchairs; 5km (3 miles) circular route.

Time: Roughly 1 hour one way; 2½ hours circular route.

Map and grid reference: OS Explorer OL7. The English Lakes – South-eastern area. Start point Rydal road car park. Grid reference 375047.

Gradients: Mostly flat. Includes some sections over 1 in 12 (shown on map).

Refreshments: Cafés and pubs in Ambleside; Pub in Rydal; Tea shop in grounds of Rydal Hall.

Toilets: Rydal Road Car Park (including disabled access); Pub in Rydal; Rydal Hall.

Getting there:

>**By car:** *Follow the A591 to Ambleside from Keswick or Windermere; or The Kirkstone Road, which links with the A592 over the Kirkstone Pass from Ullswater.*

>**Parking:** *Rydal Road Car Park (pay and display) is on the northern edge of town, opposite the college, with a dropped kerb to reach Stoney Lane.*

>**Public transport:** *Regular buses to Ambleside from all directions including from Rydal.*

About the walk

This route runs from Ambleside, in the heart of the Lake District, to Rydal, a hamlet beside Rydal Water whose name has become famous because of its association with William Wordsworth, who chose to live out his days here. Our route follows rivers and passes through woods and fields, with spectacular views of towering fells and lush valley farmland. You may want to stay by the riverside, or you could take an alternative return route through the grounds of the 200-year old Rydal Hall, on the other side of the road (note: the width and curbs of the pavement here could pose a problem for powered chairs). As part

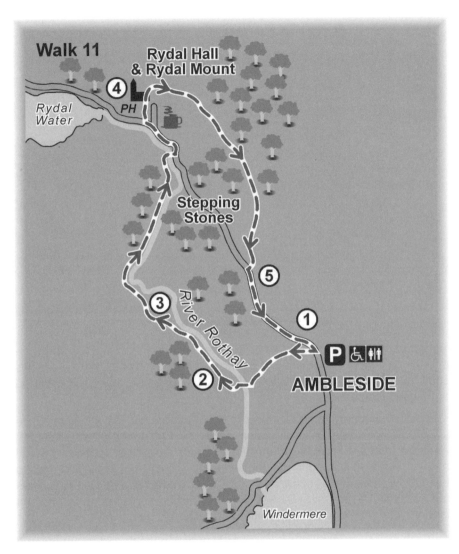

of a longer day out, you could visit Rydal Mount, Wordsworth's erstwhile home.

The route

Begin at Rydal Road Car Park (1). Turn left out of the main entrance past the fire station and police station. Take the first left down Stoney Lane and join the

The Stepping Stones are irresistible, especially to children

signed path at the end of the lane (2). The path is tarmac and flat and wide enough for a single wheelchair or pushchair. To the left of the path are views south over Rothay Park and to Wansfell; to the right is the magnificent spread of Fairfield Horseshoe.

The path runs for around 400 metres to the hump-backed Miller Bridge crossing the River Rothay (a strong pusher may be necessary for wheelchairs). After the bridge, turn right onto the quiet Under Loughrigg Road (3), which runs for 2km and is open to residential traffic, walkers and cyclists. It rises to pass through mature beech woods (look out for deer) and descends to meet the river again at Stepping Stones. The last section runs through flat pasture land and meets the A591 after Pelter bridge(4).

Turn left along the pavement and cross the road where the pavement starts on the opposite side. Please take care – the road can be busy and the pavement is narrow here and may be difficult to navigate for chairs. Up the lane on the opposite side are Rydal Church, Dora's field (filled with daffodils in spring) and Rydal Mount, Wordsworth's house.

To return you may take a slightly rougher track through Rydal Hall (5) and the pastures of Rydal Estate. This is accessible for pushchairs and wheelchairs designed for off-road use. The surface is generally good with a small uneven segment that can get muddy after rainfall. It runs for just under 2km, emerging on the A591 (5) where you can join a pavement for the last 400m to Rydal Road car park.

Optional diversion

If you're in the mood for gaining a bit of height, instead of crossing the A591 to Rydal Hall turn left, crossing the cattle grid, before Pelter Bridge(4). The single track road traces the side of the rising fell and ends at a stony track, which leads to Rydal Water. The path emerges at Loughrigg Terrace, beautifully set above the lake. Your route from here depends on your mobility – down to the lake shore along a narrow, uneven track, or straight on and yet higher to the echoing Rydal caves. The diversion to the caves, and back, adds just over 2km to the walk.

12. Raven Crag, Kentmere

Overview: Wide tarmac track with challenging gradients.

Distance: 4.8km (3 miles) return journey.

Time: 1½ – 2 hours.

Map and grid reference: OS Explorer OL7. The English Lakes – South-eastern area. Start point: grid reference 455041.

Gradients: A mixture of challenging ascents and descents, and long flat sections.

Refreshments: Tea and coffee in Kentmere in the summer season; otherwise in Staveley.

Toilets: Staveley. Accessible facilities at Wilf's Café, Staveley.

Getting there:

By car: From Staveley (accessible on the A591), follow the single road to Kentmere.

Parking: Limited car parking at St Cuthbert's Church, Kentmere, often full early in the day. Donations fund the local institute. Please be sensitive and avoid parking inappropriately.

Public transport: Buses only run to Kentmere July, August and September, weekends and bank holidays.

About the walk

Kentmere is a quiet Lakeland valley that astounds with its serenity and spectacular scenery, and is tucked away from the mainstream. Roughly 4 miles beyond Staveley and fed only by one road that reaches a dead end, it's not a place to pass through – people only come to Kentmere if they mean to spend some time here.

This linear route winds northward from the church, with the rounded tops of the Kentmere Horseshoe ahead and the River Kent ambling through the flat flood plain to the east. The tarmac track is rarely used by motor vehicles so is quiet, and although there are no benches en route, there are plenty of rocky outcrops on which to rest if you choose. The speciality of this area, as its name suggests, is its colony of ravens. They don't react well to disturbance, however, and it's important to keep away from the crags. If you're lucky, you may also see peregrine falcons. Very occasionally, red deer are also spotted nearby.

The route

Begin at Kentmere Institute (1), which sits in the shadow of St Cuthbert's Church, raised on a brow above the village and the valley beyond. With the institute on your left, follow the single track road as it climbs and curves, tracing the natural incline of the hill. If you look to your left, you'll see Kentmere Hall, still with its old defensive Peel Tower. After around 100 metres there is a gate

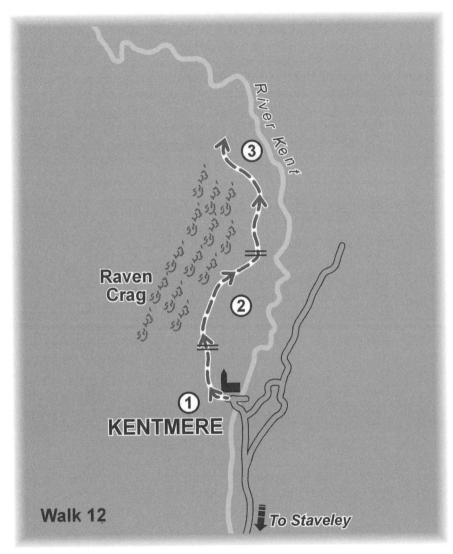

across the road. Pass through the gate, leaving the tree cover behind you, and continue uphill. This short ascent is the most challenging on the route, particularly for wheelchairs.

The road evens out after another 100 metres and there's a chance to catch your breath and take in the scenery – gentle green pastures, rocky outcrops, old hollies and hawthorns and low reedy flats around the various becks that filter into the Kent. Beyond the second gate and on the left is Raven Crag (2).

The road then bends to the right, past a farm cottage with a boisterous beck tumbling from the brackened heights behind. As you round the bend, the view opens out across the River Kent towards whitewashed cottages on the fells to the east, with Shipman Knotts cresting the ridge behind. As the road bends left again the spread of the Kentmere Horseshoe opens out ahead, with Ill Bell and Froswick to the west, High Street in the north, and Kentmere Pike to the east. The tarmac road ends at Hartrigg (3) where there is a farm. A stony track runs further into the valley to Kentmere reservoir, but this isn't suitable for wheelchairs. Instead, turn back to retrace your steps and enjoy the vista to the south.

13. Rayrigg Meadows , Windermere

Overview: Mainly gravel surfaces

Gradient: Mostly gentle inclines or level paths with steeper sections down to the lake

Distance: 1.5km (1 mile)

Time: Allow 2 hours

Map and grid reference: OS Explorer OL7. The English Lakes – South-eastern area. Starting Point: Rayrigg Meadows Car Park (1). Grid reference: 343986

Refreshments: Picnic tables and play areas.

Toilets: The toilets at the car park do not have wheelchair access.

Getting there:

By car: Rayrigg Meadows is just off the A592, 1km from Cooks Corner mini roundabout that links the A592 with the A591 just north of Windermere.

Parking: at the start of the route.

Public transport: Mountain Goat operates a Shuttle Bus service every 20 minutes that stops at the junction between Rayrigg Road and Birthwaite Road (9). Please note that the bus does not stop at the car park.

About the walk

The short walk to Windermere lake from Rayrigg Road car park is a very popu-lar trail with a winning combination of woodland, meadows and lake shores. There's also a playground, and designated picnic areas next to the car park and on the lake shore.

Rayrigg meadows is a haven for birds: great tits, blue tits, little grebes and the occasional sparrowhawk are frequent visitors here. In the early evening, Daubenton bats race across the water hunting for insects.

The car park is just below Queen Adelaide's Hill, so named after the queen herself. In 1840 Queen Adelaide, widow of William IV, arrived at Rayrigg Meadows by boat. The meadows and shoreline along this short stretch of the lake are probably much the same as they were when she alighted here in the 19th century.

A walk through Rayrigg Meadows to the shores of Windermere

The route

Your trail begins From the car park (1), looking across open fields to the lake. The view is stunning whatever the weather. The level gravel path runs for about 100 metres before bending round to the right, then continues round the base of Queen Adelaide's Hill. After around 100 metres it descends to a junction another 100 metres along (2).

Turn left here and follow the path as it meanders down through the woods to the lake shore (3). The ground is rougher and less compacted down this section but is passable with care. Oak, sycamore, beech, holly and hazel make up most of the woodland canopy. In spring and summer the ground is a magic green carpet of wild garlic, splashed with daffodils, primrose and celandine. Follow the trail along the shoreline for a further 100 metres to the open picnic area next to the jetties (4). From here the route continues along the lakeshore for another 300 metres and ends at a gate next to the Sea Scout huts (5). There are a few seats en route to take a rest and admire the views.

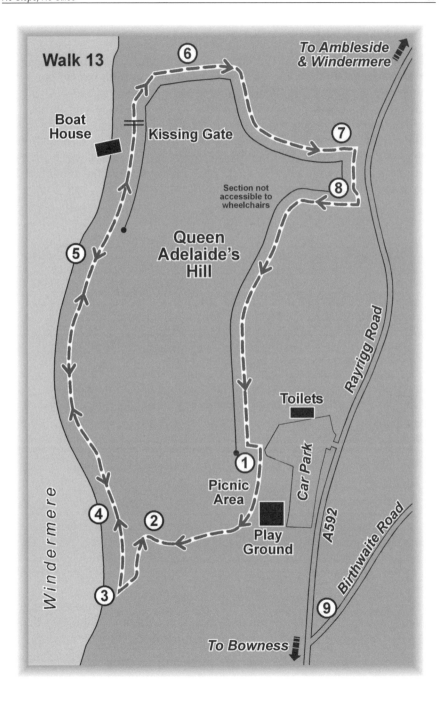

Walk 13

To Ambleside & Windermere

Boat House

Kissing Gate

⑥

⑦

⑧

Section not accessible to wheelchairs

Queen Adelaide's Hill

⑤

Windermere

④

②

③

①

Picnic Area

Play Ground

Toilets

Car Park

A592

Rayrigg Road

Birthwaite Road

⑨

To Bowness

Optional extensions

The trail continues further, but is not accessible for wheelchairs. If you're carrying on, go through the gate, and pass the boat house on your left. Continue over a small footbridge, turning right past the cottage (6) before heading up a steeper section through the woods and back to the road (7). From here turn right along the pavement for a few short steps and then immediately right again through the gate (8). The final ascent onto Queen Adelaide's Hill is about 200 metres and quite steep. The views from here across the lake are fantastic. The path continues over the other side of the hill and descends steeply down to the car park (1).

14. Red Nab to High Wray Bay: a woodland walk by the lake

Overview: Generally wide flat path suitable for accompanied wheelchair access.

Distance: 3.2km return journey on linear path

Time: Allow 2 hours

Map and grid reference: OS Explorer OL7. The English Lakes – South-eastern area. Start point: grid reference 385995.

Gradients: Flat, no gradients.

Refreshments: None – best to bring your own picnic

Toilets: None available close to the route.

Getting there

> *By car: High Wray on the west side of Windermere is about 5km from Ambleside. Follow the A593 to Clappersgate then the B5286 for about 2km then take the lane on the left signposted to High Wray. From here either walk or follow the lane down to Red Nab car park.*

> *Parking: National Trust car park at Red Nab*

> *Public transport: There is no public transport available to take you to the start of the trail at Red Nab although you can take a bus to High Wray (4) using the 505 Stagecoach service which runs between Ambleside and Coniston. From High Wray it's a really pleasant walk of about a mile on the tarmac road through Arthur Wood on the Claife Estate down to the start at Red Nab Car Park. The 505 Bus to High Wray runs quite regularly but timetables change so call Traveline - 0870 608 2608 for details.*

About the walk

Red Nab to High Wray Bay is a gentle stroll along the western shores of Lake Windermere. This is the quieter side of the lake with fine views across to high fells above Ambleside.

Windermere is England's longest lake and its most popular – visitor numbers here run into many thousands every year. So it's really nice to find a secluded place that captures the delights of this majestic lake but isn't on the main visitor routes.

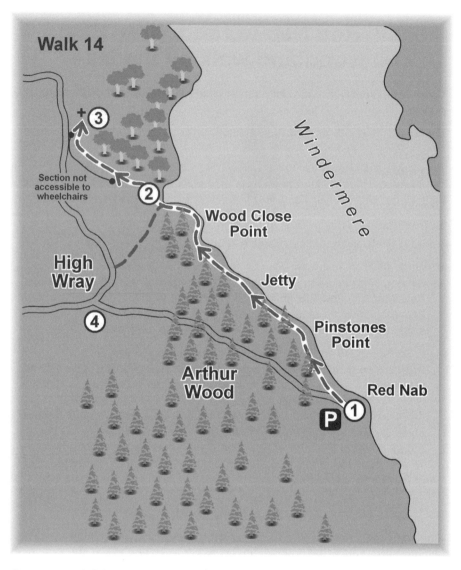

One group of visitors you won't see – but it's still nice to know they are there – are the Arctic Char. These trout-like fish spawn in the stretch between Red Nab and Low Wray Bay every autumn and are regarded as one of the lakes most important species partly because of their conservation interest but also because Windermere is the extreme south of their range. If you want to learn more about this fascinating lake and its surrounding landscape, A.D. Pickering's 'Windermere' makes fascinating reading.

Red Nab is on the edge of Arthur Wood and is part of the much larger Claife Estate which is owned and managed by The National Trust. The path is on level ground with no gradients and plenty of resting places to take in the splendid views across the lake.

The route

The route is simple to follow - from Red Nab car park (1) just head north on the lakeshore path for about one mile. Much of the trail is on the edge of Arthur Wood: oak, ash, silver birch and magnificent beech trees line the route and October/November is probably the best time to enjoy their rich autumnal colours. For the budding amateur mycologist, there's a variety of mushrooms and other fungi about too, at certain times of the year.

Looking towards the lake you will pass Pinstones, a jetty and Wood Close Point after which there is a big gate that opens on to grassy fields to High Wray Bay – which is a great place for a picnic (2). Return by the same route back to the car park.

Optional extensions

An alternative is to take a left turn from the big gate (2) for about half a mile up a very rocky path to the road (3). Low Wray Church and Wray Castle are close by. Both the church and the castle were built in 1856 by James Dawson, a retired surgeon from Liverpool. The Church was consecrated in 1861. This section is not accessible to wheelchairs.

15. Tarn Hows: Victorian lakescape

Overview: Circular walk on finely gravelled track; some steep gradients are challenging, but manageable for motorised chairs and assisted wheelchairs. The National Trust advise you to take two strong pushers.

Distance: 3km (2 miles)

Time: 1- 2 hours, depending on your pace and picnic schedule.

Map and grid reference: OS Explorer OL7. The English Lakes – South-eastern area. Grid reference 327996

Gradients: Mostly level but some steep sections.

Refreshments: Ice cream van daily from Easter to October, weekends through winter.

Toilets: None at Tarn Hows: nearest in Hawkshead and Coniston (both approx 1.5km).

Further Information: National Trust Landrover – daily Easter to October. A Self Guided Audio trail is available from the Landrover for a returnable deposit of £5.

Getting there:

> **By car:** *Take the B5286 from Ambleside to Hawkshead, then turn right for Hawkshead Hill and at the junction follow signs to Tarn Hows; or the B5285 from Coniston, turning left for Tarn Hows when you reach Hawkshead Hill.*

> **Parking:** *At tarn. The allocated accessible car park on the road in from Hawkshead Hill gives great views and access to a short path above the tarn, but does not provide access to the walk around the tarn: for this you can park at the main car park further on.*

> **Public transport:** *The Cross-Lakes Shuttle (an integrated bus and boat service) links Bowness Pier 3, Hill Top, Hawkshead, Tarn Hows and Coniston Water at weekends and school holidays (Tel 015394 45161 for timetable). On Sundays a free National Trust minibus runs between Hawkshead and Coniston via Tarn Hows. Both services run from Easter to October.*

About the walk

The high-level tarn known as Tarn Hows was artificially created in the spirit of nineteenth century landscaping by damming a beck and flooding three wet and marshy hollows. The result is that nature still dazzles you but there is a

The gently sloping grassland at the south of the tarn is perfect for picnicking

sense of design quite uncharacteristic of open countryside. To walk round the tarns – now a site of special scientific interest known for its flora and fauna – is to take a journey from one view to the next, at some points level with the water, at others above it, sometimes in thick woodland, sometimes on open grass-land. There are glimpses of small hills (the hows) and from the higher points the skyline is dominated by imposing fells – Coniston Old Man and Wetherlam to the south-west, and Fairfield, Helvellyn and others to the north. Whatever the season, it's a great route for an afternoon or morning outing.

The trail around the tarn is a favourite for families, with plenty of play opportuni-ties in water and woodland, and lots of tracks branching off from the main path. From Easter to October you can get Challenge sheets from the NT Warden to complete as you go round. The route is fully accessible for wheelchairs, though the track is rough and steep in places and may be challenging. Along the way there are plenty of benches, all with fine views.

The route

The route begins at the main car park. From the National Trust information board (1), cross the road and follow the track immediately opposite. This heads down to the southernmost edge of the tarn. Take the left branch marked

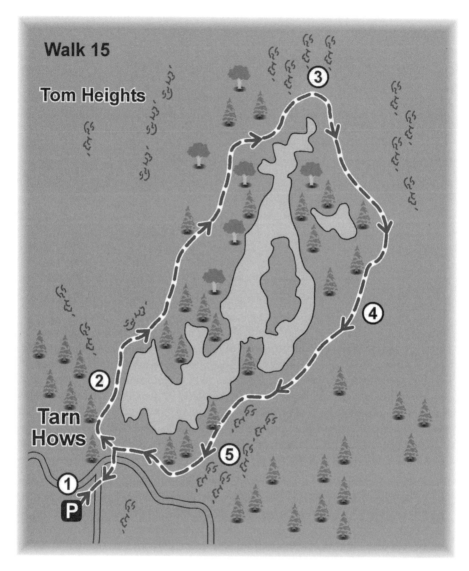

Walk 15

Tom Heights

Tarn Hows

with a small finger post to the small rough-sand beaches where children often paddle.

The track crosses a bridge (2) and continues with the tarn on your right, soon passing beneath towering trees. On your left, the land rises to Tom Heights, while on the right mature mixed woodland covers promontories and you lose sight of the lake. In bright weather, the play of light on the trees and path can be quite dramatic, while in drizzle or light rain, with the soft sound of becks dribbling into the tarns, there is a mystical feel to these woods.

The path along the western shores rises and dips before emerging from the woods at the northern end (3) where a bench is perfectly placed for a stunning view south across the water. A bridge crosses a small beck bringing the main supply to the tarn from Iron Keld and Black Crag. The path then rises at a gradient of roughly 1:3 for a few metres before entering more woodland. This is a good place to catch a profuse carpet of bluebells in spring, and there are Giant Redwoods with girths large enough to be encircled by ten or more people standing hand to hand.

For the final leg, follow the path as it emerges from tree cover (4), keeping to the lower of two tracks. You'll be 20-30 metres above the tarn with a view of the waters, islands, woodland and the fells beyond and, depending on the weather, you'll get a fresh breeze or bracing wind. The path continues, wide and flat, back to the southern end of the tarn where there is again a challenging gradient before (5) you leave the gravel track and meet sloping grass (good for picnics in summer, sledging in winter). To get back to your car, cross the grass and rejoin the original footpath for the last 10 metres.

16. Westfield Greenway: seascapes, wildlife and industrial history

Overview: Linear route on wide tarmac path accessible for walkers, wheelchair users and pushchairs. Specially designed gates at each end of the track allow motorised and non-motorised wheelchairs as well as cycles and pushchairs to come through, while barring unauthorised cars and motorbikes.

Distance: 3.5km (2 miles) one way

Time: 1½ hrs each way.

Map and grid reference: OS Explorer OL6. The English Lakes – South-western area. Grid reference: 234660

Gradients: Mostly level along the route of the old railway line. Some slight gradients.

Refreshments: Concle Inn, Clarke's Hotel at Rampside, as well as cafés at Roa Island.

Toilets: Concle Inn (not fully accessible) and public toilets at Roa Island.

Getting there:

By Car: Take the A5087 to Rampside. The A5087 links with the A590 at Barrow and at Ulverston.

Parking: There is a small car park next to the Concle Inn, with limited spaces. The parking area is on private land: please show consideration to local residents by parking within the bays only. A larger car park is available 150 metres further down the causeway at the entrance to Foulney Spit. There is informal parking close to the water treatment works where you could leave one car if you don't want to walk both ways.

Public transport: Buses from Barrow stop next to the Concle Inn at the start of the route.

About the walk

This route traces the southern Furness peninsula coastline, so you get stunning sea views to one side and glimpses into Barrow's industrial heart on the other. The contrast of timeless landscapes and modern industries is surprising and rare. If you are at all curious about Barrow's industrial pulse, the

The wide, flat path winds between grassland and the coast, which is often busy with wading birds

Westfield Greenway will give you a privileged view into some of its more modern enterprises, like the three gas terminals, and distant views of the older shipyards that were the backbone of this region. And if you're drawn to wildlife, you'll have unlimited opportunities to watch waders such as Oystercatchers, Dunlin and Redshank on the sand flats, and gulls lazing on the breeze. Or spot unusual plants in coastal marshes – sea lavender and thrift in the summer and sea aster and eelgrasses in the later months. The whole coastline is designated as a Site of Special Scientific Interest.

The walk begins where the Cumbria Coastal Way starts at Rampside. The first two-thirds are the most scenic. Towards the end the path approaches the water treatment works, whose aroma can be quite strong (depending on the prevailing wind). You can finish the walk at the car park here, or turn back and retrace your steps to Rampside. At Rampside you could extend your visit with a stroll down the road to Roa Island and a short ferry hop to Piel Island (call ahead to check ferry times and accessibility).

The route

The Westfield Greenway begins beside the Concle Inn at Rampside (1), flanked by hedgerows and passing between open fields and ponds where

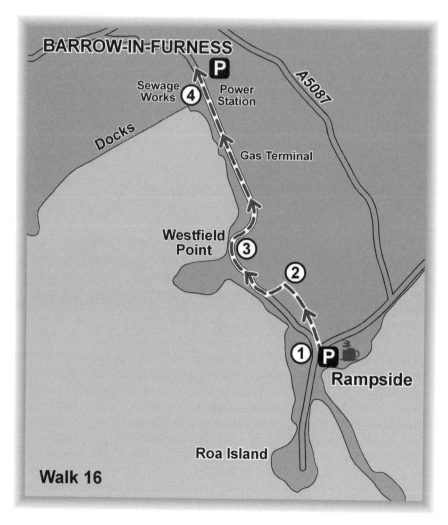

moorhens call from the reedy shallows. Initially, it follows the path of the Roa Island branch of the old Furness Railway Company line, so it is flat and straight. The trail then diverges from the railway route with a sharp left turn, clearly signed (2), and heads towards the coast, climbing to the brow of the headland. The two benches here look out across to Walney and Piel Island, so if you want a rest, now is your chance.

From here you can see the grey hint of the coastguard cottages at Walney on the horizon and, to the south-east, Roa Island and Piel Island beyond, with its ruined castle outlined against the sky. If the day is clear, you can also see landmarks along the Morecambe and Heysham shores and further south to Blackpool Tower, silhouettes of ships, and the gas rigs far out at sea. To the north-west, ahead of the path, is Barrow In Furness. The skyline is punctuated with cranes and ships in the docks, the gothic town hall and the imposing Devonshire Dock Hall.

Before long, the path brings you into view of the gas terminals on your right (3). You'll see living gas flames and an intricate maze of pipes and scaffolding – enough to get most school-aged children thinking of Thunderbirds or giant Meccano models – but not too modern for kestrels and peregrines, who make their homes here. On the left are stony beaches and the winding shoreline of Westfield Point. When the tide is out the sand flats are busy with birds like oystercatchers, sandpipers and grey plover.

The path continues along the coast, skirting around the edge of the gas terminal before passing the power station and getting ever nearer to the reservoir and docks, and closer to the water treatment works (4) and the end of the Westfield Greenway. If you have left a car at the parking spot here, this is the end of the walk. If not, turn around and head back to Rampside, with your back to the urban landscape and your face towards the sea breeze and the sky.

17. Walney Island:
where wind and sea meet the land

Overview: A refreshing coastal route on fully accessible paths. The whims of coastal weather means it's as well to dress accordingly – windy days can be bracing.

Distance: 2.5km (1½ miles) one way

Time: 1 – 2 hours there and back.

Map and grid reference: OS Explorer OL6. The English Lakes – South-western area. Grid reference: 176676.

Gradients: Flat.

Refreshments: Seasonal ice cream van midway and several pubs on the island serving meals throughout the day.

Toilets: Coin-operated toilet booth close to the Round House. Accessible toilet to the north at Earnse Point.

Getting there:

By car: Follow the A590 all the way past Barrow and on to Walney Island until it comes to an end at Biggar Bank, and Sandy Gap.

Parking: Car park at Sandy Gap, at The Round House and at Thorney Nook Lane; each has designated bays for wheelchair users.

Public transport: Stagecoach bus 1A runs from the Town Hall in Barrow Centre to Biggar Bank every 20 minutes, Mon-Sat. On Sunday the bus goes to West Shore, elongating the walk with a section that's not easily accessible for wheelchair users.

About the walk

The Walney Coastal Greenway at Biggar Bank traces the west coast of Walney Island overlooking shingle beaches, white surf and expansive seas, with views to the Isle of Man on a clear day. The sky is busy with gulls and the exposed sands and stones are playgrounds to coastal waders, including oyster catchers, cormorants and sandpipers. This area has long been a favourite of Barrovians. In Victorian times its pavilions, lidos and deck chairs bustled with activity. After its hey day the area was left to dog-walkers and families playing football on the grassy flats and looking for pebbles on the beaches. In the year 2000, with the opening of wide, flat paths accessible to all, and grass rides for horse-riders, its popularity has grown once again.

The route

Begin at Sandy Gap (1) beside the old beach-side snack bar. Facing the sea, take the path to your left. Once you have set off, there's really no chance of getting lost, and you can go at a pace that suits you. As you approach the Round House (now a restaurant) the path splits, one branch carrying straight along the coast and the other leading to the road and car parks. At the intersection you'll find the sandstone plinth that commemorates the opening of the Greenway. It's decorated with motifs designed by local school children.

Beyond the Round House there's a collection of benches (2) that are designed to accommodate wheelchairs – great places for a picnic while gazing across

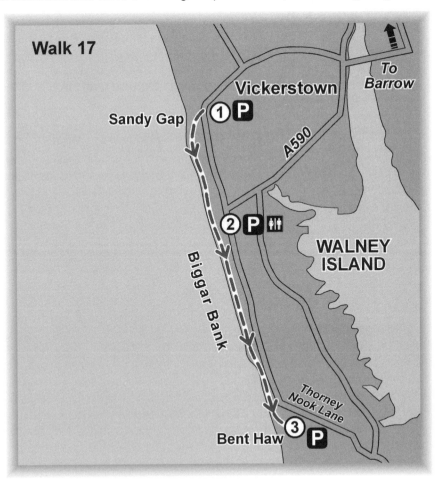

the sea to the Isle of Man. From here the path continues south, straight all the way. If there have been strong winds a very small section – about 3 metres – of the path may get brushed with sand, which adds a challenge for wheelchairs and pushchairs.

The southern part of this greenway is designated as a Site of Wildlife Interest because of specialised dune grassland vegetation. In late spring and early summer look out for the tiny flowers of the cranesbill species unique to this area. The area is also home to skylarks, which nest in the long grasses and fill the air with song in the summer. As you might expect, the path is exposed to the elements; sometimes it is blessed by sun and clear skies while the rest of the peninsula is in rain, and at other times it is buffeted by strong winds and rain coming in from the sea.

At Bent Haw, the end of the route (3), you can see for miles across the headlands of south Walney. If you are retracing your steps back to Sandy Gap you'll be able to enjoy the contrasting views of Barrow's industrial skyline to the east, the grey-blue ocean stretching to the horizon in the west, and the hills of the Lake District to the north.

Optional extensions

This route was the first Greenway established in the Furness area and may grow in the future: the Furness Greenways Partnership is exploring opportunities for extending it to the Nature Reserves at the south and north of Walney.

18. Whitemoss Common, Rydal: riverside strolling

Overview: Wide flat path.

Distance: 2km (1¼ miles) return journey.

Time: 1 hour.

Map and grid reference: OS Explorer OL7. The English Lakes – South-eastern area. Grid reference: 351065

Gradients: Flat.

Refreshments: Occasional ice cream van across road from car park.

Toilets: 40 metres from car park, with wheelchair access/baby changing.

Getting there:

By car: Follow the A591 from Ambleside, or southwards from Keswick. White Moss is roughly 4km north of Ambleside, 2km south of Grasmere.

Parking: White Moss National Trust car park, accessible from the A591

Public transport: Regular buses from Ambleside, Windermere and Kendal, and from Grasmere.

The track across Whitemoss Common on a cool winter's day

About the walk

This is an easy route and its not very long. It's a great one to know about and holds plenty of opportunities for picnicking or whiling away the hours beside the river. It's also a good route if the weather is against you – sheltered from winds and pleasant in a light drizzle – or if you don't have long but want to get out. If you're out and about with children they will love the riverside, for paddling, pebble gathering and ducks, as well as the bridges and the chance to wade through becks ... don't forget to bring wellies. The views from the path take in the river Rothay and surrounding woods, and the fells rising all around. In late spring much of the woodland floor is strewn with bluebells.

The route

Begin at the car park (1) and follow the wide path beneath the trees. You'll see marshy wetland on your left, and then you soon emerge onto flat grassland. After crossing the first bridge, there's the option of crossing the grass to the river bank. If you carry on, cross over another bridge (2) where there is also a shallow ford, much loved by children.

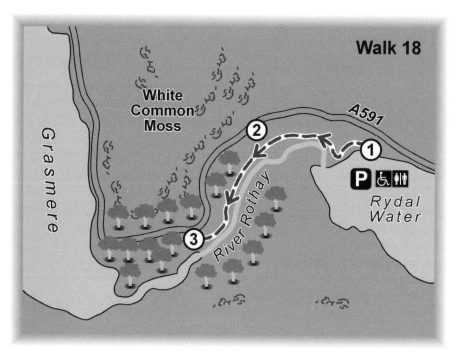

Where the path meets a stone wall, continue through the gate and straight on. (The bridge across the river here has steps at both ends.) Continue along the track until you see an outcrop of rock and a picnic bench (3), and a gap in the tree cover opening onto a tiny beach by the river: another good spot for children to play. Beyond here the path is uneven and steep, so for wheelchair users and pushchairs the route returns to the car park.

Optional extension

From the car park on the opposite side of the road, a narrow road curves upwards on its way towards Grasmere. It is steep in parts and is open to cars, but is a popular back route to Grasmere, if you wish to go that far. The distance from the car park to Wordsworth's Dove Cottage and the tea rooms on the edge of Grasmere is a little over 1km.

19. Windermere's western shore

Overview: Easy path, part tarmac and part rough track; ferry crossing included.

Distance: 4km (2½ miles).

Time: 1½ – 2 hours, depending on ferry crossing times.

Map and grid reference: OS Explorer OL7. The English Lakes – South-eastern area. Start point, Ferry Nab Car Park. Grid reference: 398959.

Gradients: Mostly flat.

Refreshments: Cafés and pubs in Bowness, plus refreshment stalls at Ferry Nab (open weekends and holidays).

Toilets: At Ferry Nab Car Park and Bowness Information Centre both with wheelchair access (Radar Key needed). Also at Ferry House on west shore (not accessible).

Getting there:

By car: Take the A592 or A5074 towards Bowness. If you're coming from the north, take a right turn to the ferry roughly 1 mile after you pass the main piers. From Newby Bridge, to the south, the turning to the ferry is on your left just after Windermere Marina.

Parking: Car parking at Ferry Nab close to the ferry landing stages on the east shore, or in Bowness; if you choose to begin on the west shore, there is a National Trust Car Park on the route at grid reference 388960.

Public transport: Regular buses to Bowness from Windermere and from Ambleside, Keswick, and Kendal serve Bowness Information Centre, and Pier 3, roughly 1km from Ferry Nab. There's also a seasonal shuttle bus (Easter – Oct) from Windermere Railway Station to Bowness. See Walk 5 for details of the path from Bowness to Ferry Nab. From the west, a seasonal Cross-Lakes Shuttle minibus runs from Hawkshead and Coniston Waterhead Hotel to Ferry House.

Boats: From Ferry Nab a car ferry crosses the lake to Ferry House every 20 minutes in daylight hours. The ferry may be cancelled in bad weather. From Easter to October, an alternative crossing to Ferry House is available on The Cross-Lakes Shuttle from Bowness Pier 3 (if you wish to cross with a wheelchair, it's essential to call in advance to check whether it is possible).

In summer, Windermere is dotted with sailing boats

About the walk

The dappled shoreline of the west shore of Windermere is quite different from its eastern counterpart. It has thick woods instead of streets and houses, and a shoreline hemmed by pebble beaches and gnarled trees that have withstood the ebb and flow of the lake for many decades. This route begins with a leisurely ferry crossing from Ferry Nab then follows the shoreline as far as Bass How. It is linear and easy, with views across the lake at every point except where the tree cover thickens. Beyond the main road, the first 1.5km follows a tarmac lane, used by a few local residents and a trickle of visitors who come to walk or to picnic by the lake. The tarmac then gives way to a stony track which is navigable by most pushchairs, assisted wheelchair users and powerchairs. Beyond Bass How the ground becomes much rougher and is no longer suitable for wheel chairs. You may want to continue if you are on foot, but we turn back at Bass How.

The route

Unless you choose to park on the west shore, your outing begins on the east shore in the Ferry Nab car park (1). The County Ferry accommodates cars,

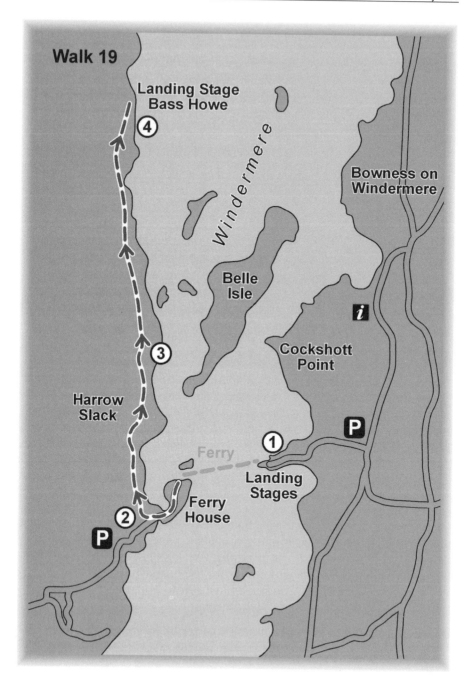

Walk 19

Landing Stage
Bass Howe
④

Windermere

Bowness on
Windermere

i

Belle
Isle

Cockshott
Point

③

Harrow
Slack

P

Ferry

①

Landing
Stages

②

Ferry
House

P

bikes, wheelchairs, pushchairs and foot passengers and the crossing takes roughly 10 minutes.

On the west shore the ferry lands at Ferry House. Follow the main road around the headland for about 400 metres. It is usually quiet but at weekends or holiday periods it does get busy, so take care. Take the first right (2) and follow the tarmac lane as it winds beneath the towering trees of Station Scar Wood. It soon emerges from the trees and cuts through the undulating grassy fields of Harrow Slack, with open views east and north across the lake, past Belle Isle. This is a popular landing place for small boats and picnickers, and a great spot for children to play.

The road continues to shadow the shore-line and meets a gate where the tarmac ends and a rougher track begins (3). The stony track is flanked by rising woodland and fern-covered ground on the left, and tree lined shore on the right. Through the trees you may catch glimpses of billowing sails, wind surfers, cross-lakes ferries and motor boats.

When you reach Bass How (4) you'll see a landing stage jutting out beyond the cover of the trees. From here there's a breathtaking view of the whale-like humps of the hills beyond Troutbeck, on the other side of the lake. Because the surface underfoot is difficult from here on, we recommend following the track back to Ferry House, enjoying southward views as you go.

Optional extension

You can extend this walk by combining it with the route featured on page 19, which follows the path from the Glebe and around Cockshott point to Ferry Nab.

20. Winster: limestone valley trail

Overview: Very quiet tarmac lane, with gates.

Distance: 9.6km (6 miles) return journey (though you could make it shorter).

Time: 1½ – 2 hours.

Map and grid reference: OS Explorer OL7. The English Lakes – South-eastern area. Grid reference 432842

Gradients: Undulating, with challenging gradient at start.

Surface: Tarmac, with grass patches in places.

Refreshments: Teas and coffees at Witherslack Old Vicarage, with outside seating.

Getting there:

> *By car: The road to Witherslack and Winster runs from the A590, midway between Levens and Lindale.*
>
> *Parking: On the road where it widens beside Witherslack School. Grid Reference 432842*
>
> *Public transport: Buses run to Witherslack from Kendal, Ulverston and Barrow every hour Mon-Sat, and infrequently on Sundays.*

About the walk

The Winster Valley is one of South Lakeland's well-kept secrets, dearly loved by those who know it. It's a classic limestone valley, overlooked by the craggy and wooded sides of Whitbarrow Scar on its eastern side and spreading in hillocks and hollows beyond the River Winster towards gentle fells in the west. The valley is quiet and serene most of the year and bursting with the energy and exuberance in spring: the trees are budding, the daffodils bobbing, the birds are busy, the lambs are bleating and there are calves suckling. This route follows a quiet road on the eastern side of the valley, slightly raised above the flood plains of the River below, passing farms, pastures, woodland and many limestone features, including ridged outcrops and old kilns, once part of active quarry sites. The route sticks to the road but it's extremely quiet – used only by local traffic to a handful of properties.

The route

Begin by Witherslack's Dean Barwick School (1), where there is reasonable space for parking along the road side. Head north along the road towards the

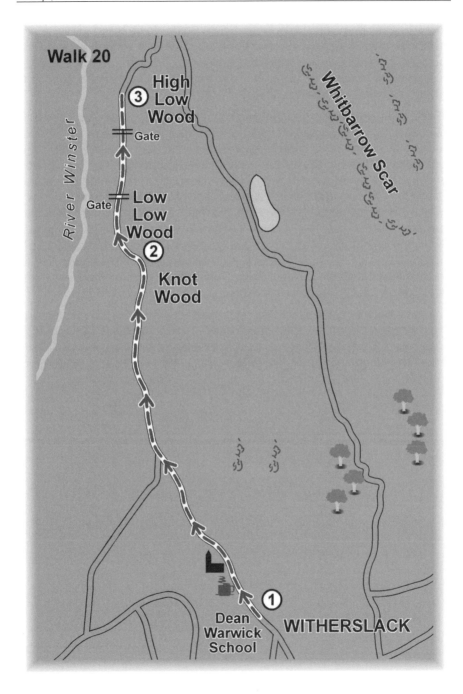

churchyard, with its staggeringly tall yews. Before long the road drops and there's a downhill stretch, which may be a challenge for manual chairs and pushers. Take it slowly and look into the woods on the left – there's a lime kiln here with a distinctive arch. As the road flattens out you'll get a chance to appreciate views across the valley.

After a quiet stretch, the road passes a disused quarry on the right and then reaches a farm and some cottages. Beyond this the lane is flanked by fields and scattered woodland, dotted with limestone features. At Knot Wood (2) the road bends sharply to the left between mature hedgerows. You can tell how quiet it is here by the stretch of grass down the middle of the road. The road curves right to meet the dwellings of Low Low Wood. Beyond this there is a gate. It is not stiff but the latch is high and unaccompanied wheelchair users may have difficulty opening it. On the other side, you'll soon see Middle Low Wood on the right. The road curves gently upwards, giving increasingly inspiring views as it does. On a clear day you can see beyond Gummers How to some of the central Lake District Fells. There's another gate before you reach High Low Wood (3) the brow of this gentle rise and the end of the walk.

The route back to Witherslack School is via the same road, but the peace of this valley and the equally good views on return over stretches of the Winster to the hills of Staveley-in-Cartmel and High Newton more than make up for the repeated ground and the challenging push towards the end. A sip of tea or coffee in the lovely gardens of the Vicarage is a great way to finish.

21. The Bowder Stone

Overview: To the Bowder Stone – the route is suitable for wheelchair access and is of compacted gravel.

Distance: Less than 1km in total.

Time: Allow 2 hours.

Map and grid reference: OS Explorer OL4. The English Lakes – North-western area. Grid reference 254164.

Gradient: A little steep over first 150 metres then gentler inclines to the Bowder Stone.

Refreshments: Grange village is less than 1km north along the B5289.

Toilets: None close by.

Getting there:

By car: Take the B5289 about 9km from Keswick and less than 1km from Grange.

Parking: There is a large National Trust car park at (1) on the east side of the B5289.

Public transport: The Borrowdale Rambler is a regular service operating between Keswick and Seatoller. From Easter to October the No. 77 and 77A (Honister Rambler) connect with Keswick.

About the walk

The Bowder Stone is one of the most popular visitor attractions in the Lakes. This 400 million-year-old andesite rock stands over 10 metres high and its 30 metres circumference is balanced precariously on one edge. People have been know to crawl underneath and shake hands with someone on the other side – a bit scary with 2000 tonnes of rock above you. There are wooden steps to the top of the boulder, which offers great views of Borrowdale valley and surrounding fells.

While you're there you could visit Quayfoot quarry or take a stroll through the woods to the shores of the River Derwent, both a short hop from the car park.

The route

To the Bowder Stone: From The National Trust's Quayfoot Quarry car park (1) follow the track to the access path leading to the Bowder Stone (2). The path is of compacted gravel and in generally good condition. The first 150 metres are

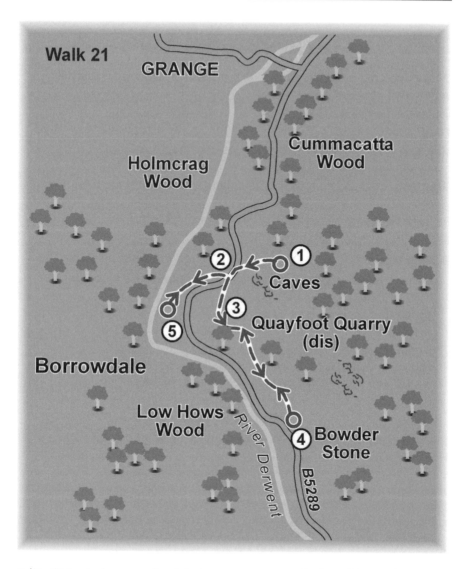

Walk 21

GRANGE

Cummacatta Wood

Holmcrag Wood

Caves

Quayfoot Quarry (dis)

Borrowdale

Low Hows Wood

Bowder Stone

River Derwent

B5289

quite steep and some wheelchair users may need a hand here. Follow the path upwards and then to the left, where you will see an abseiling platform (3). From here bear right and continue through woodland rising gently for a further 200 metres to the Bowder Stone (4). There are plenty of benches scattered about so you can simply sit back and take in the splendour of this gigantic geological phenomenon.

The Bowder Stone is over 400 million years old and weighs over 2000 tonnes

Optional extensions

To the caves: Take a few minutes and wander into this industrial heritage: plants and animals have started to re-colonise the area as nature begins the slow process of reclaiming its own after years of slate quarrying. Go through the gate next to the path at the start of the walk (2). From here carry on for about 150 metres to the Quayfoot Quarry caves (just below (3) on the map). There is no access into the caves but there is a real sense of history here. Watch out for the occasional visitor dropping in from above, for this is the base of the abseil, described earlier!

Through the woods to the river: Cross the road at (2) and follow the trail through woodland for about 150 metres descending gently to the banks of the River Derwent (5). It's a little muddy in places but generally firm. This is a quiet, tranquil place looking out across to Holmcrag Wood on the western shores of the river.

22. Cat Bells

Overview: Wide flat path.

Distance: 1km linear path (2km return to car park).

Time: 1 – 2 hours.

Map and grid reference: OS Explorer OL4. The English Lakes – North-western area. Start point: grid reference 247212.

Gradients: Mostly flat, with gentle to moderate inclines in places.

Refreshments: Bring your own or the closest facilities are in Portinscale about 2.5km north.

Toilets: None near the route.

Getting there:

By car: Take the B5289 heading west to Portinscale. Follow the minor road signposted to Swinside. Before Swinside, turn left towards Hawes End.

Parking: There is parking near Skelgill, just above Hawes End, grid reference 247212.

Public transport: Timetable: No. 77A & 77 (Honister Rambler) runs between Keswick and Cat Bells four times a day from Easter to October.

About the walk

The Cat Bells terrace walk has great views of lake and mountains without the struggle of a strenuous uphill climb. It also runs parallel to another of our Easy Miles walks along the western shores of Derwent Water (Trail 23).

The road takes you to about 50m vertical height above the western shores of Derwent Water and from here the whole of the lake stretches out before you.

It's one of those places from which you can do a little landscape feature spotting. Castlerigg Fell, Bleaberry Fell and High Seat are over to the east and just in front of you is St Herbert's Island. In Beatrix Potter's 'Tale of Squirrel Nutkin', squirrels can be seen paddling across Derwent Water to St Herbert's Island. Beyond is Rampsholm Island and to the north is Derwent Isle and beyond is the busy market town of Keswick. Over to the south you can easily pick out Lowcrag Wood and the craggy outcrop of Surprise View, which is close to the picturesque Ashness Bridge.

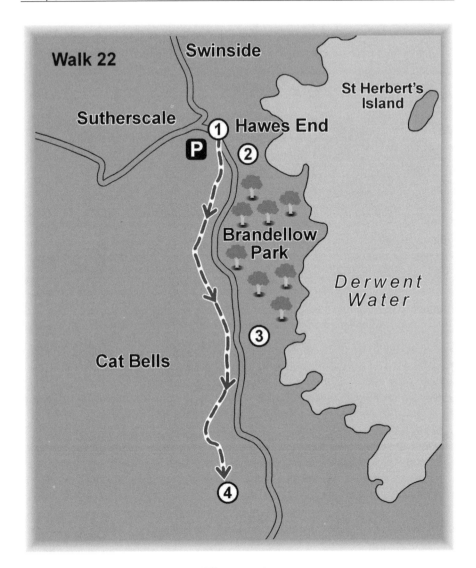

The route

From Skelgill car park (1) (grid reference 247212), walk back along the road for about 30 metres then follow the road right for another 40 m. Avoid the first trail which is the main route to the top of Cat Bells. Instead, take the second path (2) on the right hand side of the road which runs above and parallel to the road.

Fine views across Derwent Water from Cat Bells terrace

The path has been completely restored and is in very good condition. The first section rises at a moderate incline for about 40 metres and is the only challenging part. After this the route levels out for about 400 metres before sloping down to a small car park by the side of the road (3). From here the trail rises again on a varying gentle-to-moderate incline before levelling off. A further 400m will bring you to a memorial stone (4) dedicated to a former Keswick resident, Sir Hugh Walpole, who wrote the Rogue Herries Chronicles – a fictitious saga about a Lake District family (you can see his original manuscripts in Keswick's Fitz Park museum). Situated above Manesty Park, this is a great place to take in the views.

Optional Extension

Beyond the Memorial is a bridleway and footpath, which eventually drops down to Manesty Park. This extension to the route is unusable for wheelchair users but could be navigable with an off-road push chair.

23. Derwent Water: Hawes End to Manesty Park

Overview: Generally wide flat path with several gates suitable for wheelchair access.

Distance: 4km (2½ miles) from Hawes End to Manesty Park return.

Time: Allow 1.5 hours

Map and grid reference: OS Explorer OL4. The English Lakes – North-western area. Start point: grid reference 247212.

Gradients: Mostly flat, with gentle inclines in places.

Refreshments: Bring your own or nearest is in Portinscale.

Toilets: None near the route.

Getting there:

By car: Take the B5289 heading west to Portinscale. Follow the minor road south for about 2.5km. Before Swinside, turn left towards Hawes End.

Parking: There is parking near Skelgill, just above Hawes End grid reference 247212.

Public transport: No. 77A & 77 (Honister Rambler) runs between Keswick and Cat Bells four times a day from Easter to October.

Boats from Keswick: There is a regular service from Keswick to Brandelhow in the summer season. Call Keswick Launch Company 017687 72263 for information (www.keswick-launch.co.uk).

About the walk

This trail runs along the west side of Derwent Water from Hawes End to the road junction at Manesty Park. What sets this route apart is its collection of sculptures – one of them 'Entrust' is a wooden hand dedicating 100 years of the National Trust's work at Brandelhow. It runs parallel to the Cat Bells Terrace trail described earlier (Trail 22).

The path also passes two landing stages so you can take the motor launch from Keswick to Hawes End landing stage, walk to High Brandelhow landing stage and enjoy a leisurely boat trip back to Keswick.

The National Trust now owns much of the surrounding land and has done an

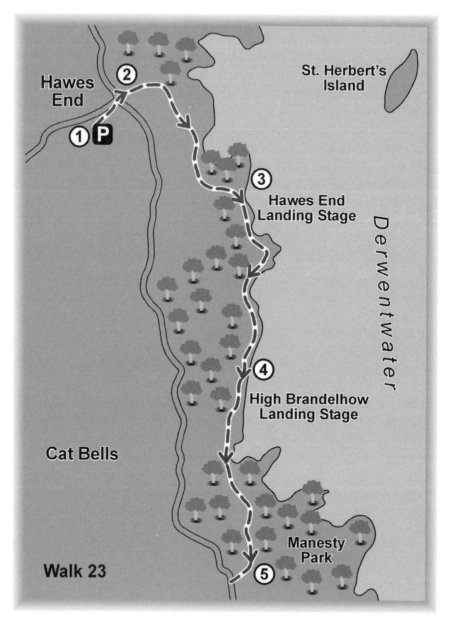

Hawes End

① P

② St. Herbert's Island

③ Hawes End Landing Stage

④ High Brandelhow Landing Stage

Cat Bells

⑤ Manesty Park

Walk 23

Derwentwater

impressive job restoring the footpaths and reinforcing the embankment to protect tree roots and natural vegetation from erosion.

The route

The linear route takes you from Hawes End in the north to Manesty. It's about 2km long. Park at Skelgill car park (1) grid reference 247212 and walk back along the road to Hawes End Education Centre (2). Here, the trail is sign-posted towards the lake and meanders through open grassland and woodland to the Hawes End launch landing stage (3).

There are sheep on the grasslands and the woodlands contain a rich variety of oak, birch, hazel and chestnut – deer are frequent visitors here. Follow the path along the lake shore for about 1km to High Brandelhow landing stage (4) – the ENTRUST hand-sculpture is in this section. There are plenty of places for a picnic and great views east across the lake to Falcon Crag and Brown Knotts. Continue around the bay and into Manesty Park for about 0.5km where the path eventually joins the road (5).

Optional extensions

You could take a leisurely cruise from the Derwent Water landing stage at Keswick to Hawes End (3). From here it's about 1km along the lake shore to the High Brandelhow landing stage (4), from where you can get another boat back to Keswick. For wheelchair users there is a ramp onto the jetty although access on and off the boats is limited.

24. Force Crag Mine:
walking back through time

Overview: Compacted gravel suitable for accompanied wheelchair access

Distance: 8km (5 miles)

Time: Allow 3-4 hours

Map and grid reference: OS Explorer OL4. The English Lakes – North-western area. Starting Point: at car park (1), grid reference 228236

Gradients: Inclines for the first 1km then generally flat for 3km to Force Crag Mine

Refreshments and Toilets: None on the route but there are pubs in Braithwaite village

Getting there:

By car: Take the A66 from Keswick to Braithwaite then the B5292 through the village towards Whinlatter Pass. The walk starts at the sharp right angle bend about 1km out of the village.

Parking: Limited parking at the start of the route (1). Further parking spaces are available 1km further up the Whinlatter Road

Public transport: The X5 runs between Keswick and Braithwaite roughly every two hours in both directions. From Easter to October the 77/77A (Honister Rambler) runs between Keswick and Whinlatter four times a day.

About the walk

This walk takes you to Force Crag Mine, now an ancient monument but once the heartland of a thriving mining industry.

Situated at the head of Coledale Valley, the mine is one of several old abandoned workings scattered along the lower reaches of Long How and Force Crag, about 4km south-west of Braithwaite. Workings in this area date back to the sixteenth century. Since the 1830s mineral deposits of lead, zinc and barite have been mined and processed here for use in the glass, paper and chemicals industries. Force Crag was active as recently as 1991; it was the last working mine in the Lake District.

In recognition of its historical significance, the site has recently become a scheduled ancient monument. The National Trust, with funding from the National Lottery, has undertaken essential works to make the site safe and

Walking into Coledale Valley towards Force Crag Mine, now an ancient monument

has restored some of the more interesting archaeological features. The processing mill is open to the public on certain days through a booking system. Contact The National Trust on 017687 74649 for further information.

The route

Follow the Whinlatter Road out of Braithwaite and park at the old quarry about 500 metres from the village (1). The route follows the old mine service road. It is a little rough and steep for the first 1km but then levels out for the rest of the journey. It's a further 3km to the mines (2). As you go, you'll get glimpses of Causey Pike towering over the craggy outcrops of High Force and Crag Hill. The valley itself is flanked by the gentler shapes of Sleet How and Low Moss fells, vibrant with colour in summer and autumn. Coledale Beck runs through the middle of the valley and completes this naturally sculptured Lakeland landscape.

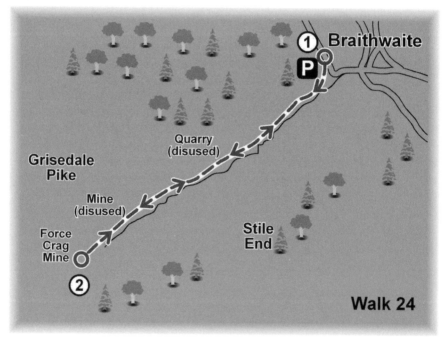

At the mines, the remnants of the old brick and tin processing house, conveyor belts, gantries, rusting machinery and spoil heaps present a different sculpture. These ramshackle old buildings tell a story of human endeavours – a valley full of people and a once vibrant industry that contributed to the local economy and the working culture of the Lake District.

Follow the trail back to Braithwaite.

25. Friar's Crag, Derwent Water

Overview: A circular route on easy paths, taking in fabulous lake shore.

Distance: 3km (2 miles)

Time: Around 1 hour; but lots of potential for picnicking and staying longer.

Map and grid reference: OS Explorer OL4. The English Lakes – North-western area. Start point: grid reference 266229.

Gradients: Mostly flat, a few very slight gradients.

Refreshments: Café by the lake shore; more in Keswick.

Toilets: Car Park, accessible.

Getting there:

By car: *From Keswick pick up the road to Borrowdale (B5289) and almost as soon as you leave Keswick turn right at the roundabout towards the lake. The Theatre and car park are clearly sign posted.*

Parking: *Pay and display car park by Theatre on the Lake.*

Public transport: *Buses from all over Cumbria. The main bus station in Keswick is 700m from Hope Park.*

About the walk

Derwent Water is a spectacular lake, fringed by pebbly shores and framed by grand mountains. This route gives a taste of both: gentle shores where you can rest, play and picnic, and breathtaking views across the water to the hills beyond. It also takes you through woodland, which is deliciously fresh and colourful in spring, summer and autumn, and may be laden with snow in winter. There's also a chance of getting out on to the water if you'd like to, with rowing boats for hire (not winter) and a cross-lake ferry service that visits the shore near Lodore Wood and Fawe Park on the west shore.

The route

Begin at Hope Park (1) and head down the road towards the lake shore. The route follows a wide tarmacked lane, where there are some picnic tables, and then enters the shade of the trees. To the right of this lane is the pebbly lake shore, which is easy to get over with most pushchairs and with powered wheelchairs. From here you can pick up a rowing boat or hop on the ferry if you'd like. For this walk, however, continue along the shore and up a ramp, which joins with the tarmac lane. The lane ends and a narrower path continues

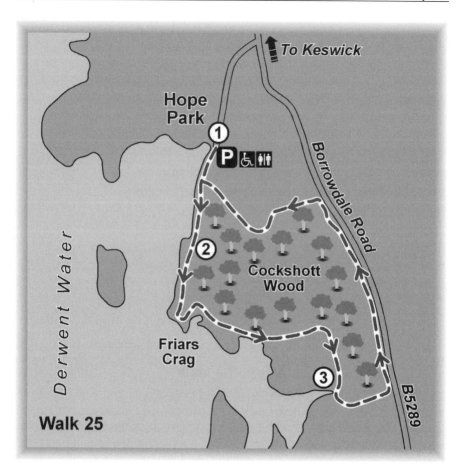

beneath the canopy of the trees. Between them, you can see the lake, the island, and the stepped humps of Cat Bells on the opposite shore.

You'll soon come to a fork in the path (2). Take the right 'fork' and carry straight on: this takes you to Friar's Crag, which boasts what must be one of the finest views across the grey-blue waters of the lake towards the Jaws of Borrowdale. There's a bench here. If you have a chair, you'll need to retrace your steps from here back to the fork and take the left branch to go on. If you are walking, you can skirt round the edge of the crag and follow some steps to rejoin the path.

The path passes through a gate and out of the trees to cut through a spread of smooth grass that runs up to the water's edge. This is a great spot for a picnic,

The pebbly shore en route to Friar's Crag is a popular launching pad for rowing boats and the small cross-lake ferry

for kids to play, or just for sitting and enjoying the space. When you're ready to move on, the path winds into the woods and then meets a wider track (3). At this point, turn left. Follow the track towards the road (B 5289). Just before it meets the road your path branches left, dipping beneath the trees and then running parallel to the road for about half a mile. Then take the first left: the path takes you into Cockshot Wood. When you get to the woods, turn left again, and then choose the first right turn. You continue through the woods, carpeted with delicate white wood anemone in late spring and early summer, and emerge back at the lake shore by the jetties.

Optional extension

This route begins beside Keswick's Theatre by the Lake, which boasts a huge range of performances and exhibitions by local and national performers and artists. There are also beautiful gardens and ponds and a pitch and putt course at Hope Park, right opposite the car park.

26. Keswick railway: the tracks of time

Overview: Linear route, easy surface, several access points, small section at one end unsuitable for wheelchairs. The path is also used by cyclists.

Distance: 5km (3 miles) one way. You can choose shorter sections.

Time: Roughly 2 hours to walk the full route, one way; 4 hours both directions; options for shorter walks along the same route.

Map and grid reference: To start: OS Explorer OL4. The English Lakes – North-western area. Move to OS Explorer OL5 to finish.

Gradients: Mostly flat but short section of gradient over 1:12 (around 18%) at Threlkeld end: possible but not advisable for accompanied wheelchair users.

Refreshments: Keswick Leisure Pool. Threlkeld if you are walking further.

Toilets: At Keswick Leisure Pool, with wheelchair access.

Getting there:

> **By car:** *Drive into Keswick on the A66 (from Penrith or Cockermouth) or the A591 (from Windermere and Ambleside). Follow the signs to the leisure pool, on the northern edge of town near Fitzpark.*
>
> **Parking:** *Keswick Railway Station; 3 spaces mid-route on the Brundholme Road.*
>
> **Public transport:** *No bus stop at Keswick Leisure Pool. There is a stop at 'County Corner' 500 yards from the start of the walk. Buses run between Keswick and Threlkeld, around 500 metres from the end of the walk, roughly every hour, less frequently on Sundays.*

About the walk

This fabulous walk follows the old Keswick railway line beside the River Greta between Keswick Spa and the A66 at Threlkeld. It passes through woodland, cuttings and fields, giving vistas of some of Keswick's sentinel fells. It is maintained by National Park Rangers, in conjunction with local land owners and Allerdale council, and there's plenty to see in terms of wildlife, including king-fishers, if you're lucky, and red squirrels, who boldly hang out at their personal feeding station. Despite proximity to major roads, there's very little traffic noise.

For children, the highlights might be the old bridges – 7 in all – and trip-trapping over the boardwalk snaking round the hillside. For others the draw may be the

Part of this fabulous route is a walkway winding through ancient beech trees

Greta, and the dippers and herons playing across her surface. The Greta is one of the most important rivers in the north of England, a SSSI, home to otters, herons, kingfishers, dippers, trout and salmon, and the main feeder to Bassenthwaite Lake.

The route

This walk can be started at several points. For clarity, we start at Keswick Leisure Pool. Alternative access points are marked in the text and on the map.

Begin from the car park just past Keswick Leisure Pool (1), behind the old station (now part of Keswick Hotel). The wide track runs up to and beneath Brewery Bridge and the A 591. It then trails up to the imposing concrete Greta Bridge that carries the A66. Turn around and take a look back: if the weather is clear you'll see a range of hills west of Keswick, including Causey Pike and Grisedale Pike.

After the bridge the path crosses a field and joins the slatted wooden board-walk (2) that skirts around the hillside through beech woods, with views to the River Greta below. At the end of the boardwalk the path slopes down to rejoin the old railway track and soon meets the site of Low Briery Campsite. There's an optional drop-off point here (3) with wheelchair access, but no public park-

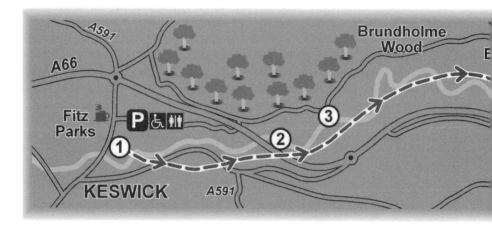

ing. This is also the site of an old bobbin mill, busy in the early part of last century and now remembered by the foundations of a station platform. You can catch up on the history from an information board.

The track continues, very flat, between mature woodland and steep cuttings, with open views across the river at intervals. After the next bridge there's a narrow footpath with steps down to the riverbank that snakes back to Keswick through Brundholme Woods – this is an option for walkers. The main path continues through open countryside, with views over the treetops to Lonsdale Fell and Blencathra.

Soon there is an access point for wheelchairs (4) that joins Brundholme Road and parking for 3 or 4 cars. Brundholme Road is quiet and you could continue along here to Threlkeld if you wish. On the main track, there's a shelter, with a bench and information boards on the River Greta. The track then passes through a tunnel, and then, after a short distance, crosses a cast iron bridge where the Greta meets Glenderaterra Beck.

Further along is another shelter (5), with a seat and information boards about the railway. The track continues to a cast iron bridge with gates. On the far side of the bridge is a squirrel feeder (6), where, with luck, you may watch red squirrels. After this the track becomes rougher and steep as it joins the cycleway on the edge of the busy A66, en route to Threlkeld. It's not suitable for wheelchairs but is an option for cyclists and walkers.

Wheelchair users may leave the track at point 4 or go on to the squirrel feeder (6) and then return to Keswick. For walkers a narrow, rocky path, with steps in places, branches off the main track before the last bridge, and follows the Greta beneath the A66. The path crosses a minor road and then joins the old

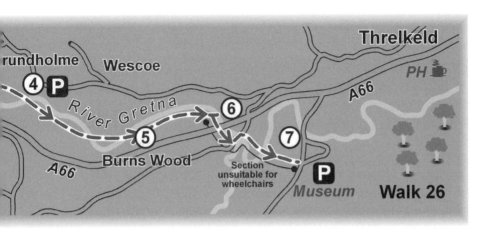

rail route that once led to Threlkeld Station, where there's a car park (grid reference319246) (7). The Mining museum nearby is a great draw for children.

Optional diversion

You can join this route and leave at several places. The main diversion, accessible on foot but not with wheelchairs, is the path to Castlerigg stone circle, one of the most celebrated and photographed of Cumbria's stone circles and superbly placed for views at every point of the compass. The path to Castlerigg begins where the River Greta meets Glenderaterra Beck (just before 5 on the map). For this diversion, add roughly 45 minutes each way.

27. Loweswater

Overview: Quite wide, flat path suitable for accompanied wheelchair access as far as Watergate Farm.

Gradient: Flat and smooth.

Distance: 1.5km (1 mile) linear path from Maggie's Bridge (2) to Watergate Farm (3)

Time: Allow 1½ hours for the 3km round trip.

Map and grid reference: OS Explorer OL4. The English Lakes – North-western area. Start Point: grid reference 135210.

Refreshments: None available although the Kirkstile Inn in Loweswater village serves refreshments and excellent home-brew beer (6)

Toilets: None en route – Kirkstile Inn is the closest and has accessible toilets.

Getting there:

By car: From Cockermouth take the B5292 for about 3km then bear right along the B5289 through Low Lorton for about 3km. Bear right again for about 2.5km. Before reaching the lake take a left turn (1), signposted to Watergate Farm.

Parking: Leave your car at The National Trust car park near Maggie's Bridge (2). Parking for those with limited mobility is available at Waterend Farm (3).

Public transport: There is a dial-a-ride bus service 949 operating between Cockermouth, Lorton, Loweswater and Buttermere on Monday to Saturday. Contact 01900 822795 to make a booking and for further details. Summer bus services vary.

About the walk

Situated on the north westerly edge of the National Park, Loweswater has a timeless, tranquil quality that makes this route so appealing. Loweswater doesn't attract high visitor numbers because it is outside the busy tourist areas, but the path around the lake is a local favourite.

The lake itself is only a mile in length and about half a mile wide but is set in an impressive and varied landscape. Looking beyond the southern shore is the rugged shape of Melbreak Fell and in the distance stands Grassmoor and the magnificent Whiteless Pike. Views to the north reveal an open landscape

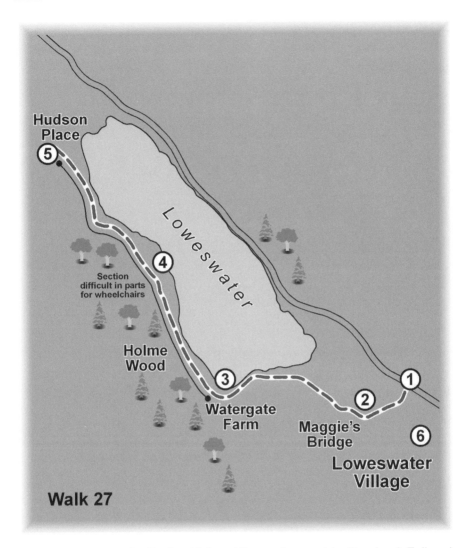

Walk 27

flanked on the east by Darling Fell and the on the west by Burnbank Fell and Carling Knott.

The National Trust owns the lake and much of the surrounding land and, for those who feel the urge to get back to nature, the Trust's Holme Wood Bothy is available for hire. Or, if you fancy a row on the lake, boats can be hired from Waterend Farm which is on this route – call 01946 816940 about both the bothy and boats.

Taking in the views en route to Loweswater

The route

The walk starts at The National Trust car park near Maggie's Bridge (2). Walk through the gate and follow the lane towards the lake. There are open fields, hedgerows and dykes on either side of the path with great views of surrounding fells and the lake straight ahead. The shoreline is fringed in parts with healthy reed beds and lily pads that provide a perfect habitat for insects, birds and other wildlife. The path is level and in good condition all the way to Watergate Farm (3). This is a lovely place to stop and take in the views before returning to Maggie's Bridge by the same route.

Optional extension

For the more adventurous, the path continues through Holme Wood, a wonderful mix of mature oak, birch, beech and conifers that stretches along most of the western fells. You may see red squirrels and will pass the Holm Wood Bothy (4), before reaching Hudson Place (5) where there is another car park, near Waterend. But please note that the path from Watergate Farm to Waterend is rough in places and there are a few ups and downs and at least one small stream to negotiate. Accompanied wheel chair users might find this section difficult.

28. Mirehouse Trails: playgrounds and strolls

Overview: A combination of tarmac, compacted gravel and loose gravel. Most paths are suitable for accompanied wheelchair access.

Distance: 3km (2 miles)

Time: Allow 2½ hours – more if you spend time in the playgrounds or picnicking.

Map and grid reference: OS Explorer OL4. The English Lakes – North-western area. Starting Point: Entrance to grounds (1). Grid reference: 234282.

Gradient: Mostly gentle inclines from Bassenthwaite Lake back to Mirehouse with a few steeper inclines.

Refreshments: Old Sawmill Tearoom opposite the entrance to Mirehouse Toilets. Dodd Wood car park, including accessible toilets

Contacts: There is a charge for entry. Contact 017687 72287 for details of access arrangements and group bookings.

Getting there:

> **By car:** *Mirehouse is located on the A591, east of Bassenthwaite Lake about 5km north of Keswick and only 4km from Bassenthwaite village.*

> **Parking:** *Old Sawmill Tearoom at Dodd Wood car park – opposite the entrance to Mirehouse.*

> **Public transport:** *The 73, 73A and X4 go to Mirehouse from Keswick on the A591. Timetables change with the seasons.*

About the walk

Mirehouse is a wonderful old 17th-century house with a variety of walks within its grounds. There are plenty of options to choose from – short walks, long walks, nature trails and history trails, all set in a landscape of woodland, pasture and formal gardens. The adventure playgrounds are a particular favourite with small children.

A walk among ancient Scots pine, larch and oak woodland, plus plenty of flowering shrubs, fruit trees and open parkland with stunning views across Bassenthwaite lake, a perfect way to while away a lazy day.

MIrehouse is teeming with wildlife. The most celebrated visitor is the rare osprey that can be seen plying the lake for fish during the spring and summer.

Owls and buzzards are often seen here. Red squirrels, which are becoming increasingly rare in the UK, also live in these woods.

The route

There are many trails to choose from and most are linked so you can move across different routes, depending on what captures your interest.

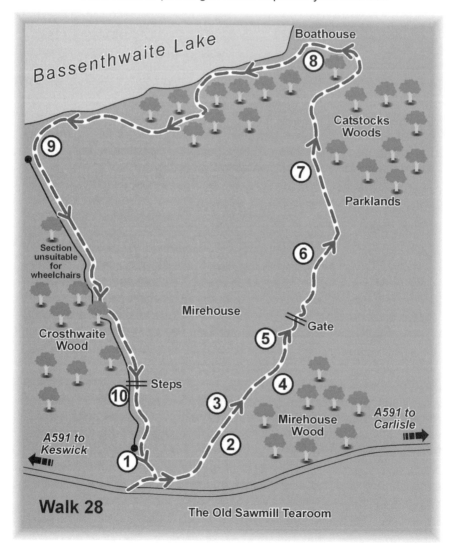

Starting at the entrance to the grounds (1), follow the tarmac lane for about 200m. Branching off from this are two play areas – (2) and (3) on the map – with forest castles, a steeplechase, swings, rope ladders and a zip wire for the more adventurous.

Returning to the tarmac and gravel road, turn left. After 150m the road forks (4). Turning left takes you past the main house (5) and through a gate to another lane. Turning right another gate (6) leads to a path across open park-land and in to Catstocks Wood (7).

Optional extension

An alternative route from the fork in the path is to follow the signs for Lakeside Walk, which meets the other route at the gate (6) leading to Catstocks Wood – This section is not suitable for wheelchair users. From (7), follow the path around to the boat house (8) and out of the woods along the shores of the lake – this is a lovely place to stop for a picnic. Follow the path for another 150m and turn left (9) through Crosthwaite Wood, over a tarmac lane and back to the entrance (1). There are a few medium-steep gradients (over 1 in 10) and four steps on this last section.

Playtime on the Mirehouse Trail

29. Mungrisdale: a country lane

Overview: Unadopted tarmac road suitable for accompanied wheelchair access.

Distance: The round trip from Mungrisdale to Scales and back is 10km (6¼ miles).

Time: Allow 3 hours

Map and grid reference: OS Explorer OL5. The English Lakes – North-eastern area. Start Point: The Mill Inn, Mungrisdale. Grid Reference: 362303.

Gradient: Generally quite flat but some short steep sections.

Refreshments and Toilets: None en route. Refreshments are available at The Mill Inn (Mungrisdale) and The White Horse (Scales).

Getting there:

> **By car:** *From Threlkeld follow the A66 for 5km and turn left on to a minor road for 3km to Mungrisdale.*

> **Parking:** *No official car park but the roadside doesn't have many parking restrictions.*

> **Public transport:** *The X4/X5 operate between Penrith and Keswick stopping at Scales and Mungrisdale road end. The Caldbeck Rambler No 73/73A runs less frequently from Carlisle, calling at both Mungrisdale and Scales en route to Keswick.*

About the walk

This is a very pleasant secluded route along an unadopted road linking Mungrisdale and Scales, 3km north of the A66 between Troutbeck and Threlkeld.

This picturesque part of Cumbria offers a variety of walks along quiet country lanes – and this is one of the best. The road is tarmacked and gated: few vehicles use this lane although you can expect to see the occasional cyclist as it is part of the Coast to Coast (C2C) cycle route.

Heading out from Mungrisdale to Scales the route is elevated with a few farms and houses along the trail. What's particularly interesting is the marked contrast between the bracken-covered fells above the road and the cultivated grasslands and fields on the lower slopes.

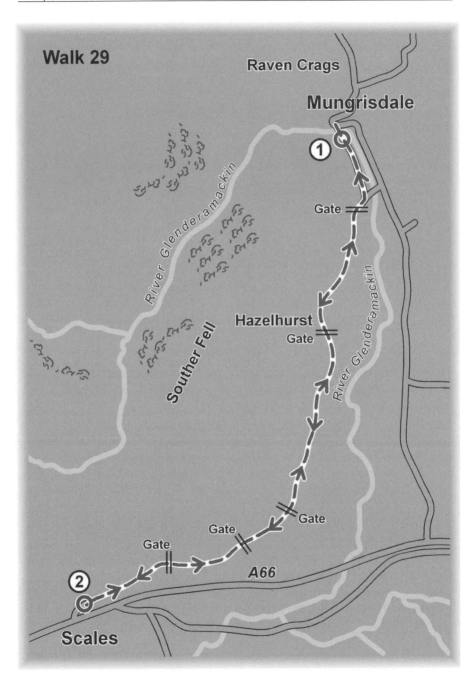

A pleasant stroll down a quiet country lane at Mungrisdale

The route

The route is generally flat although there are several steep sections where the lane meanders around a number of small becks running off the fells.

Starting at The Mill Inn in Mungrisdale (1), there are wonderful views looking east across to the distinctive cone-shaped Great Mell Fell and to the south to Matterdale Common, Great Dodd and Clough Head. The lane runs parallel with the River Glenderamackin. This remarkable river starts its long descent on the upper reaches of Blencathra and its track forms almost a full circle behind Souther Fell before it joins the River Greta en route for Derwent Water.

A few hundred metres beyond The Mill Inn, the lane moves away from the river, rising slightly, and begins its contour around Souther Fell, Mousthwaite Comb and Scales Fell, crossing small becks running off the fells. After this, it's mostly downhill to The White Horse Inn at Scales (2). Returning by the same route means that it is a little steeper, particularly the first section out of Scales.

30. Patterdale: Grisedale trail

Overview: Tarmac lane with short steep section leads on to rough unmade road.

Distance: 1.5km (1 mile) linear route (3km return)

Time: Allow 2½ hours round trip.

Map and grid reference: OS Explorer OL5. The English Lakes – North-eastern area. Start Point: grid reference 391162.

Gradients: One steep section of about 250 metres, gentle slopes for a further 500 metres – the rest is generally level with only minor gradients.

Refreshments: Glenridding and Patterdale

Toilets: Glenridding and Patterdale

Getting there:

> **By car:** *Grisedale Bridge, Patterdale is on the A592 at the southern end of Ullswater.*

> **Parking:** *Public car park in Glenridding 1km from the bridge (cars do park on the side of the lane by Grisedale Bridge).*

> **Public transport:** *Stagecoach 108 service runs from Penrith to Glenridding and Patterdale 5 times a day . The 517 runs from Ambleside to Patterdale and Glenridding in the summer.*

About the walk

Our walk follows Grisedale Beck from Patterdale at the southern end of Ullswater. Surrounded by some of the biggest mountains in the Lake District, the views from this valley walk are spectacular.

Not surprisingly, this is a popular starting point for some of the most challenging walks in the area, including Helvellyn, the highest mountain in this part of the Lakes.

But it's not just the big mountains that draw people to this part of the Lake District – the gentle valley walks have their attractions too – Glenridding, Glencoyne and Aira Beck with its impressive Aira Force waterfall can all be reached from the A592 that follows Ullswater's north-west contours.

A gentle walk along Grisedale's beck, surrounded by some of Lakeland's biggest mountains

The route

The walk starts at Grisedale Bridge off the A592 opposite the Police and Fire Station at Patterdale (1). The tree-lined tarmac lane is level for about 300 metres and then turns right and rises steeply for another 250 metres to Close Cottage (2). Most wheelchair users will need assistance on this section. From here the lane continues to rise, but less steeply, for a further 500 metres before levelling off.

Go through the gate (3) and follow the lane past conifer plantations – Peppercorn Plantation on your left. From here the path opens up to reveal the wide gentle slopes of Grisedale valley. To the north are the steep sided Grisedale Brow and Bleaberry Crag; St Sunday Crag with its Chockstone Gullies are to the south and the dramatic Dollywaggon Pike, Nethermost Pike and Eagle Crag form the head of the valley to the west.

The track descends slightly and follows the beck closely. There are plenty of places along this section to stop and take in the fabulous views.

After a further 500 metres or so the lane changes from tarmac to unmade rough stone and gravel and becomes a little rougher under foot (4). The

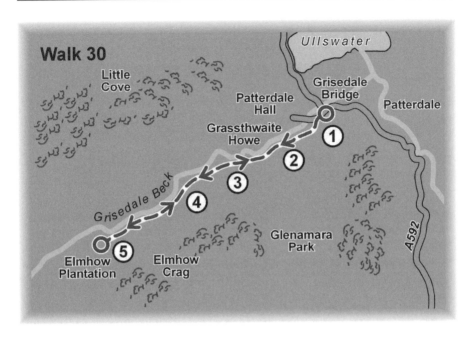

options are to continue towards Elmhow Plantation (5), which simply takes you a little further into the valley, or to rest here before heading back down the same route.

31. Revelin Moss:
a walk in the woods

Overview: Wide flat path

Distance: 3km (2 miles) circular path

Time: Allow 1½ hours

Map and grid reference: OS Explorer OL4. The English Lakes – North-western area. Start point: grid reference 209242.

Gradients: Mostly flat, with gentle inclines in places.

Refreshments: Visitor Centre, open daily 10.00am – 5.30pm with shop and refreshments: there's a children's play area and other trails start from here.

Toilets: At the Visitor Centre, including accessible facilities.

Getting there:

By car: From Braithwaite follow the B5292 for about 3.5km and turn left into car park.

Parking: Revelin Moss Car Park or the Visitor Centre on the other side of the road at the Forestry Commission's Visitor Centre.

Public transport: Timetable: No. 77 & 77A (Honister Rambler) runs between Keswick and Whinlatter four times a day from Easter to October.

About the walk

High up on Whinlatter Pass, Revelin Moss is a really beautiful place to take a gentle stroll and admire the views. In the valley below you will see the River Derwent and Bassenthwaite Lake, flanked along its northern shores by the towering Skiddaw mountain.

Revelin Moss itself is about 300 metres (1000 feet) above sea level and sits at the foot of Grisedale Pike. It was here in 1919 that the newly formed Forestry Commission planted its first conifer plantation in the Lake District. Today this particular section of the Commission's Whinlatter Forest is being allowed to revert to its natural state. Conifers are giving way to semi-natural woodland of oak, ash and rowan trees with natural grasses, ferns, moss and wild mountain flowers spreading out along the banks of Grisedale Gill.

There is an excellent Visitor Centre across the road, including an exhibition

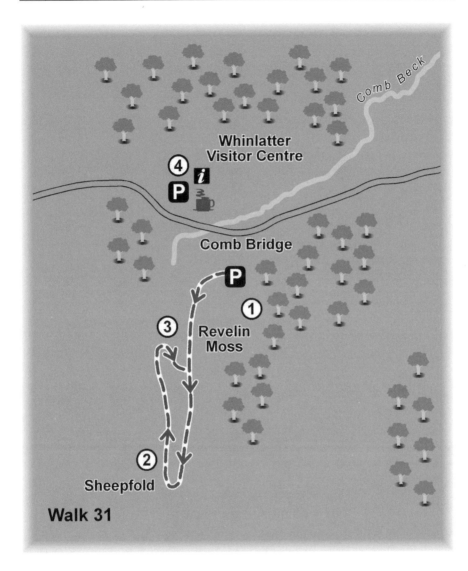

Walk 31

centre where you can learn about the local wildlife and the celebrated ospreys that nest close by; see overleaf for further details.

The route

The path starts at a car park just opposite the Forestry Commission's

Time for a rest and to take in the views from Revelin Moss

Whinlatter Visitor Centre, in Thornthwaite Forest about half-way up Whinlatter Pass (1). The outward southerly leg of the journey follows Grisedale Beck and there are magnificent views of Grisedale Pike rising steeply to an impressive 791m (2570 feet) above sea level. There is a gentle incline for 1.5km to a bench in a clearing that lures walkers to rest and enjoy the views (2). From here the path falls gently for about 1km before crossing Grisedale Beck (3) and then rejoining the outward path for the last 200m to the car park (1). If the weather's clear on this last section you'll be rewarded with great views to Thornthwaite Forest.

Optional diversion

Across the road, about 300 metres from the Revelin Moss car park, is Whinlatter Visitor Centre, with a shop, refreshments and children's play area. A number of other trails start from here (4), although theses are not suitable for wheelchair uses. There's also an exhibition centre and visitors can watch live CCTV coverage of the famous osprey's nesting site. This magnificent but badly persecuted bird of prey is a must to see. Fledglings usually leave the nest in mid August.